CITIZEN SURVIVOR'S HANDBOOK

CITIZEN SURVIVOR'S HANDBOOK

Prepared by
Steve Hart &
Richard Denham

Foreword by
Cody Lundin

Illustrations by
M. J. Trow

Issued by
The Ministry of Survivors

This edition published 2016 worldwide by T Squared Books.
www.tsquaredbooks.co.uk

Copyright © 2016 Steve Hart and Richard Denham

A CIP catalogue record for this book is available from the British Library

ISBN: 978-0-9954521-7-6 (paperback)

All rights reserved including the right of reproduction in whole or in part in any form. The moral right of the author has been asserted

T SQUARED BOOKS

During the 1940's Britain suffered a national catastrophe that would become known as 'The Great Tribulation' by its survivors. The remnant of His Majesty's Government formed a department known as The Ministry of Survivors, the mandate of this office being to help, guide and inform the public through the anarchy around them. During the early years they produced and issued a handbook known as 'The Citizen Survivor's Guidebook'.

However, as the situation became more desperate, the guidance within this book quickly became redundant. The Ministry deemed that the only remaining course of action was to produce a second edition; informing people to evacuate the chaos of the towns and cities and flee to the countryside, focusing on wilderness survival and how to be self-sufficient on the move.

This is a surviving copy of that handbook.

MINISTRY OF SURVIVORS

ABOUT THE AUTHORS

STEVE HART
Steve Hart is one of the Britain's top survivalists who specialises in wilderness survival. He is a lead figure in the 'prepping' community which plans for various potential disasters and how to live through them.

Steve also writes for the *Bushcraft & Survival Skills Magazine* and authors several websites including www.keepcalmandsurvive.co.uk

RICHARD DENHAM
Richard Denham is the author of the *Britannia* series of books, co-written with best-selling author M. J. Trow. *Britannia* is set during the fall of Roman Britain and the descent into the Dark Ages. Richard specialises in British propaganda and his other books include *Weird War Two*.

www.britannia-series.co.uk

ILLUSTRATIONS
Internal illustrations by M. J. Trow.

Confound their politics
Frustrate their knavish tricks
On Thee our hopes we fix

GOD SAVE US ALL…

CONTENTS

1. Do's
2. Don'ts
3. Words and Phrases
4. Rule of Threes
5. Introduction
6. Shelter
7. Water
8. Fire
9. Food (in the wild)
10. Hygiene, sanitation and first-aid
11. Weapons and defence
12. Signalling and communication
13. Food (in Shangri-La)
14. Journey's end

FOREWORD

In the early 1940's, Britain was paying a heavy price for refusing to bow to Nazi Germany. 'The Blitz' destroyed more than one million London homes and killed more than 40,000 civilians. Several British cities were attacked multiple times in bombing raids that spanned eight sleepless months.

In all survival situations, advance preparation is key. One man - Winston Churchill - had been warning his country and the rest of Europe about the Nazi war machine as early as 1933. The backbone of being able to survive emergencies is psychological. It's the ability to take into account and prioritize all available resources. Yet not all resources are physical, and the survivor must also bring forth and push forward positive mental and emotional stamina to endure and survive. Through the fog, fear and chaos of war, Churchill rallied the British people again and again to bring forth and push forward their very best. In the end, through inspired leadership and resourcefulness, the Nazi bombing campaign failed to demoralize the British people.

All life threatening scenarios are terrifying to the people going through them. It can't be any other way. However, with the correct training, the right mindset, or what some refer to as 'luck', people do survive emergencies. It's my hope that with proper survival training and inspiration gleaned from *The Citizens Survivor's Handbook*, that the reader will become more self-reliant in an always changing world. In the words of Churchill, 'Never give in, never give in, never, never, never, never – in nothing, great or small, large or petty – never give in except to convictions of honour and good sense.'

Cody Lundin
Professional survival instructor and best-selling author of 98.6 Degrees: The Art of Keeping Your Ass Alive and When All Hell Breaks Loose: Stuff You Need to Survive When Disaster Strikes.

DO'S

DO remember you are a still a British citizen and a subject of The Crown.

DO stay alert at all times.

DO be firm but fair with others you come across.

DO avoid talking about the old days or deluding yourself things will go back to normal.

DO keep people at a distance, even with those with whom you have regular contact.

DO steer clear of all disputes that are not your own.

DO wean yourself off tobacco, chocolate, tea, coffee and alcohol; there won't be any more anytime soon.

DO remember that female company, though appealing, will likely result in having to deal with hysteria, venereal disease and unwanted pregnancy.

DO stay out of trouble.

DO give dilly-dalliers a wide berth.

DONT'S

DON'T trade in sterling, it's only good for fire fodder; only barter with essential items.

DON'T be sentimental. If things are tough for bully denizens and townies they have only themselves to blame.

DON'T believe other people's accounts of Britain's current situation. They have deluded themselves with false ideas based on misinformation and propaganda.

DON'T fall for hard-luck stories or agree to a travel companion unless it is of benefit to yourself.

DON'T be taken in by compassion for former friends, neighbours and co-workers. They are not the same people they once were.

DON'T trust anyone in a uniform, they are not following official orders and the MOS cannot and will not be held responsible for their actions.

DON'T be tempted to join the Church of the Remnant. They are charlatans and rogues.

DON'T panic!

WORDS AND PHRASES

Bindle – Not an actual bindle mind. A collective term to describe the various bags and ruck-sacks that are the Citizen Survivor's best friend. It can also loosely refer to everything in your possession or you have access to.
Bug in – To 'hunker down' and be at a fixed location, this is fine by MOS guidelines as long as you are not in an urban environment.
Bug out – To be on the move and leave a fixed location. Recommended for all townies.
Bully denizen – Folk who are well beyond the pale. Those mischievous brigands with no regard for the old laws who wouldn't think twice about giving you a thump to save their own necks; avoid at all costs!
Citizen Survivor – That's YOU!
Lord Wind-bag – Earl Wathmere, that mad old fool, we have included an excerpt of his bizarre rambling broadcasts for the purposes of showing you what a nonsense this man truly is.
Church of the Remnant – Odd chaps indeed, dunce cap-clad wrong 'uns who are a couple of slices short of a meat pie, keep well away!
Doolally – To lose your marbles, go insane.
Jack Jones – Hero of the popular radio show, 'The Adventures of Jack Jones'. A series of public service announcements by the Ministry of Survivors.
Keep mum – Stay silent, reveal nothing about your

size, location, situation, supplies or intentions about yourself or any group you are with to anyone. Don't ask others either. Careless talk costs lives.

Moaning Minnie – Grumpy defeatist sorts.

MOS – His Majesty's Ministry of Survivors.

Scrumping – Scavenging and foraging for food and supplies.

Shangri-La – Your end destination (you'll know it when you find it).

Townie(s) – Folk(s) who still live in urban environments.

Wailing Winnie – (see Moaning Minnie)

RULE OF THREES

Extreme weather can kill you in just 3 minutes
No water can kill you in 3 days
No food can kill you in 3 weeks

INTRODUCTION

"They that dwell on the earth shall wonder, whose names were not written in the book of life from the foundation of the world, when they behold the beast that was, and is not, and yet is."
– Revelation 17:8-10; Church of the Remnant

Firstly - A very warm welcome, Citizen Survivor

A very warm welcome to you sir (or madam). First of all, congratulations for reading this book. We don't know how you came across it, whether honestly or in slightly fishy circumstances but that is not our concern; what is important is that you are reading it.

This is the second edition of the handbook for Citizen Survivors, aimed primarily at townies and former townies and to guide them through the daunting task of escaping their urban environments. We advise chucking any first editions on the fire as they are outdated and the information provided within will give you lots of false hope and misinformation.

This book has been produced with the backing of His Majesty's department, the Ministry of Survivors and we hope it is of some use to you.

We have been specifically instructed not to provide any information about the bigger picture as there is simply no way to know how things will go, and any information given may already be outdated by the time you read it. We could sit here all day lamenting what has been or could have been, but that's not helping anyone. We'll all end up as useless and hysterical as women if we go down that road!

For now, the Ministry of Survivors simply hopes you can stay alive. The popular The Adventures of Jack Jones radio show was another MOS tool to communicate useful information but there will be no further episodes of that, though we have chosen to include several excerpts of it for your information.

For you and your loved ones to stay alive you need to get out of town, learn to survive in the wild, and hopefully find your own Shangri-La somewhere out there, but it will be a long and dangerous journey and you must keep your wits, resolve and a good old stiff upper lip if you want to avoid going doolally.

Although we appreciate this is a contradictory statement coming from a government department, we strongly recommend you do not engage with, or even make yourself known to anyone who appears to be acting in an official capacity on behalf of His Majesty. There is no chain of command now, soldiers, police officers, wardens and other uniformed bodies will not be acting on our behalf, and we cannot be held responsible for their actions. Simply keep mum, stay quiet and out of sight of these dubious folk.

We hope you can appreciate our frustration at having to provide such vague advice on some issues, and having to omit so much information from the first edition, but as everyone appears to be in such different situations, what was useful for one is now misleading and possibly even damaging to others.

Therefore, we shall do our best to stick to our official directive as ordered by the Ministry of Survivors, simply to try to keep you and your loved ones alive and hopefully encouraging you to not fall in with any bad apples.

Incidentally, we strongly recommend you do not try to make contact with the Ministry of Survivors and stay out of London! Nothing good can come from this city now.

A last point, we have an extremely complicated relationship with the Church of the Remnant which we will not go into. However, we strongly urge you to avoid these folks at all costs, because, however despairing you are at the moment, it's nothing compared to what lies down that path.

It's going to be a long and dangerous road and we truly understand what a daunting prospect this is for diehard townies. Remember though, you shouldn't fear the unknown any more than you should fear what is going to happen to you if you stay put! Keep on reading and you'll eventually be as lucky and crafty as Jack Jones himself.

Get your head down, stay strong, keep your nose clean, keep mum and avoid all contact with strangers. We wish you luck and as always, hope for the best and plan for the worst!

Chin up, cheerio, carry on!

- *The Authors, on behalf of HRH's The Ministry of Survivors*

Common questions

Why can't I just stay put in town?

For obvious reasons we do not recommend continuing to inhabit the towns, the buildings may seem warm and dry but you do not know what structural condition they are in. Worse than that, bully denizens fester in urban environments; if you're lucky, you'll be dead meat when a few of these ne'er do wells get you, assuming they aren't too sadistic. If you're unlucky, they'll just steal your bindle, probably condemning you to a slow and painful death.

The average Citizen Survivor probably used to very much be a town dweller and has probably rarely ventured out into the countryside, except perhaps for a romantic liaison with an old flame. But for the Citizen Survivor who should have a bug out plan already in place, survival skills are an essential part of your preparation for the world today.

Hopefully you will follow MOS guidelines and leave any urban environment immediately. Townies are not your friends; you are competing over the same limited resource, and past experience has proven how ugly that can get! There may be the odd cad who scrapes by in the towns, but they are not people you want to cross, and they won't want to cross you either.

If you're still having your doubts and think you're safer in a town, here are a few things to knock some sense into you.

- Townies have too much to lose and too much to defend – themselves, their families, their base and their supplies – you may think you can scare off any bully denizens and give them a bloody nose, but it's a war of attrition and you're only delaying the inevitable.
- Women folk are particularly reluctant to move on and 'bug out'. Remember, women are emotional creatures, particularly if they have children, and you will need to be stern with them and be the voice of reason. It's for their own good!
- Women are devious creatures and will feign affection for you if it means keeping themselves alive. If you are naïve enough to fall for their honeyed words you will have the burden of looking after another stranger, who will desert you as soon as someone bigger and better comes along.
- Women are naturally disposed to being mothers, they will use tricks and their womanly wiles to convince you to sleep with them. A pregnancy is most likely a death sentence for the mother and babe, though women will not have the rational mind to understand this under any circumstances. They also carry venereal disease.
- Animals such a dogs soon become wild and feral – they will be desperate for food and could well form packs – if you cannot defend yourself you'll ending up being their supper. Even if you somehow outrun these packs of dogs there's a high chance of developing a fatal disease from a bite.

- The unbearable truth for townies really begins to sink in when the reality of having no food hits them. They will be forced to find their own food and beg, borrow or steal to get it. Worse still, they will be searching out rancid, discarded food, simply to help stop their hunger. Do not expect charity from anyone, if you're not self-sufficient you are a liability and will soon find yourself with a bloody nose or worse.
- There are even worse potential acts that may be undertaken by the really desperate and those willing to do so; cannibalism. There are many recorded cases of people staying alive by eating the meat from dead bodies. If you find yourself eating other folk, by golly you've lost it!
- There will be disease and potential life threatening viruses and pathogens lurking in every bin and old food container you uncover.
- The towns have no infrastructure, they are tombs!
- Under these conditions it is not surprising so many townies reach a state of panic, if not total psychosis, as they desperately search for food and water.
- Townies go through all sorts of mental distress as their bodies slowly begin shutting down as the advanced stages of dehydration begin to set in
- Undoubtedly townies will have to go through unbearable personal trauma when their family are suffering with intense hunger pains and water dehydration.
- Lack of personal hygiene and washing facilities

will lead to all sorts of infective skin rashes. As personal hygiene reduces townies will be opening the door to all sorts of germs.
- Townies' lack of storing and storage space, even such simple, essential items as toilet paper, will increase the rate of personal problems and disease.
- Insect bites soon infect those that find themselves looking for food and water in bins.
- With no additional medical supplies and no first aid skills or training, townies won't have a clue about treating any sickness that will inevitably catch up with them
- Their lack of medical supplies leaves their loved ones sick and dying – all for the lack of a good supply of disinfectant!
- Loved ones who simply cannot take it any longer frequently commit suicide. Nothing can ruin your day faster than that. Bad news!
- Townies see people all around them lose hope and any sense of belonging in civilised society. They will start to act like wild animals, resorting to any means to stay alive.
- All rational thoughts will be put aside and give way to barbaric, wanton hunger. It will not be long before townies end up devouring the family dog or cat.
- There will come a time when the frightened townie simply has to venture outside in search for food and water. In advanced stages of hunger and dehydration, the risks are very high. These pitiful folk end up becoming completely disorientated and confused, they'll end up

getting lost and finally collapsing with exhaustion.
- Lack of vitamins and nutrition along with dire conditions sinks everyone into fits of depression and despair.
- Townies often suffer from 'the heebie-jeebies', where they simply become paralysed with fear and terrified of the outside world. This, as you can imagine, is its own death sentence.
- Remember, trust no one, uniforms mean nothing. Many a time has a desperate townie revealed themselves to a squaddie or a copper, only to be rounded up like strays and never seen again. We don't know what they're up to, but we bet you and your family won't like it!

Remember Citizen Survivor – The cavalry aren't coming, no one is going to rescue you. Keep your chin up, cheerio and carry on!

We cannot overstate the deplorable violence that townies give and receive. If a townie ventures out unarmed it would be a bloomin' mistake. If they think they will not encounter bullies and violence from others more hell bent than they are on getting some food, then they should think again.

So? Have we convinced you to get out of town? We sure hope so, otherwise you've had it. Now, it's time to 'bug out', pack up your troubles in your old kit bag and become a Citizen Survivor! Good luck!

How do I know when to 'bug out?' (From the first edition)

DISCLAIMER: Please read the next section carefully, Citizen Survivor. We have carefully considered whether to remove it or not from this edition. We have left it in for posterity. However, as you know; the situation has changed drastically since the first edition. So read the following with a large pinch of salt (assuming you can get hold of any)!

What's the best time to bug out? Or do you just bug in? What would it take for you to leave your home and just go?

Well, it would take a lot, we assume – it would have to be on the absolute point of a confirmed death situation to bug out.

Bugging out sounds easy, in fact, to some people it's what they think they have to do.

Hold on tiger – Bugging Out is the absolute, very last solution to staying alive. Why would you want to just up and leave the safest place you know, especially when you have spent so much time preparing your home for survival? You've probably spent thousands acquiring everything you need, all under one, safe roof – and you're going to just up and leave!?

Bug in facts
- You know your home, your surroundings, your neighbours – it's your turf.
- You know the exact amount of provisions you have – you can calculate your survival time.
- Your family are familiar with your home and

surroundings.
- You have a set plan to protect your home, with ample and varied weapons.
- You have all the resources you need, prepped and ready to use.

The simple truth is that Bugging In is a far better plan for long term survival and we would never recommend considering bugging out unless you feared for your life.

Bug out facts
- How do you get to your bug out location – on foot, bike, horse, boat?
- Is your bug out location safe?
- Do you even have a bug out location?
- You must have supplies already cached, along the way and at the safe location
- How long can you survive there?
- How prepared are you for a long term bug out?

The truth is, you must have several bug out plans.

The next most important thing to do is practise, practise, practise. Rehearse for as many scenarios as you can, test yourself and make improvements each time – don't leave anything to chance.

And, of course, ensure your family takes part and is prepared.

If and when to bug out is a very serious decision to

have to make. Prior to any bug out decision you must have an escape plan and bindle ready and waiting to go. One important factor in your bug out preparation is the choice of your bindle and what's in your bindle. Each survival situation is different and requires a different plan and survival preparation. As always the key is to be fully prepared for bugging out. The final choice is with you to make the decision to bug in or bug out and it may not be that easy.

Oh what a different time it was back then! It is painful to read back the advice from the first edition. However, I'm sure you'll forgive the MOS for its naïveté and realise that bugging out from any urban environment really is the only option now.

Where should I go?
Good old Blighty has some fantastic areas of natural beauty and unspoilt open spaces, with thousands of acres of wilderness to get lost in within our national parks. From the Cairngorm hills and mountains of Scotland, right down to the harsh and exposed wilds of Dartmoor and Exmoor, you are never too far away from unspoilt solitude. They're all away from civilisation, and that is where you want to be.

Remember though, Citizen Survivor, you must never attempt to go out into the wilderness unprepared. It is essential to know the top survival skills needed to ensure you will be able to keep yourself alive should something go pear shaped.

There are several golden rules, each as important as the other, but you must follow them – preparation is key. When you do eventually build up the courage to flee the towns, consider the following.

- Make sure you are fit enough to do what you think you can do!
- Gain as much 'classroom' knowledge of Citizen Survivor skills as possible.
- Practice your survival skills at home and in the garden.
- Plan, check and the double check your routes, times, rest points and camp. Don't get caught out without a camp when the sun goes down!
- Keep mum! Do not tell anyone when and where you are leaving, where you are going or even what direction. This can lead to all sorts of mischief. Careless talk costs lives.

Your end goal is your own Shangri-La, only you will know when you've found it. A little secluded cottage in a Welsh valley? An abandoned manor house in the Scottish Highlands? A shack by the sea? This is for you to decide in good time.

What should I take?
Just what equipment you do and don't carry with you is a matter of individual choice, but again, there are some important bits of kit you really cannot do without:

- A means of collecting and purifying water for drinking.
- A means of making a fire for cooking.
- A good quality and large bindle.

- Ordnance map / compass / torch / knife.
- Waterproof clothing / spare socks / hat / good walking boots / poncho.
- A copy of this handbook!
- Tarp.
- Tent / bivvy / hammock etc.
- Suitable sleeping bag.
- First aid kit + first aid booklet with emergency first aid.

This list can go on and on – but remember, it's personal choice – if you were well trained in survival you need very little to get by, but for most of you it's a case of pack as much as you can comfortably carry.

You will never learn until you actually go out and do it. Learning how to survive in the wild is an essential skill that must be mastered in order to go out and be confident that you will survive. Fortunately, here in Blighty we have a predictable and a relatively mild climate for most parts of the country. Unlike across the pond in the US of A where there are levels of extremes far in excess of that in the UK.

Should I travel abroad?
[Omitted by order of the MOS]

What should go in my kit bag?
Of all the kit that you'll need for a Citizen Survivor, the absolute number one is a good decent kit bag (bindle)! Bet you didn't think a bindle would be top of the list did you? Well, there is egg on your face now, my lad.

As young men we all thought that 'more equipment was better' however, we were fitter and stronger then! We could carry our own body weight, and still have the strength to carry a bit more. But, now we've all got that bit older and supposedly, that bit wiser, we realise it's far more about your skills than your equipment. Having the knowledge to live off the land and survive means having to rely on less gear. That means you have to carry far less in the first place. So learn your Citizen Survivor skills and know how to survive off the land using minimum equipment – this will make packing your bag far easier when it comes to choosing what to take and what to leave behind.

Firstly, give some thought to the equipment that is essential to you – your bindle is obviously essential, as are things like a decent knife, mess tin and even good fitting boots! – These items are 'must haves' and will keep you going without anything else.

When it comes to your bag, weight is one of the biggest factors – you will be walking for some time and over a long distance, negotiating rough terrain and the more weight you carry the higher the risk of injury – the amount of weight will also effect the speed at which you can cover ground.

It is highly unlikely you will be able to carry more than an 80l bindle for any distance – assuming you can actually get it on your back in the first place. So don't try, the object is to get away from danger and cover ground fast.

Most people can handle a 60l bindle. You should be able to pack just about everything you need into one of these bindles – they were designed for the military with comfort and survival for soldiers on the move in mind.

Deciding to 'go big' and choosing a 80l+ bindle can be a big problem – unless you're trained and constantly practise, you will not be able to move fast enough. If you have no choice but to walk, you must be prepared with a suitable sized bindle. Bag size is very important, as you may well be required to get out fast and put distance between yourself and whatever danger you're moving from.

Bring knives, lots of knives. But why we hear you ask, when one good knife will do? Think about this – a penknife will not split (baton) wood into smaller pieces for a fire, but it will skin a rabbit far easier. A bigger knife will baton wood and won't snap the blade

Place your bag on the ground, and then give it kick – if you're worried you might break something inside, then that bit of kit does not belong in your bag! You have to be fully prepared for breakages and damage and the rough terrain ahead of you. Similarly, if you land and end up hurting your foot, then the pack is just too bloody heavy. It will weigh you down, make you slow and fatigued and too immobile; this will be so tempting to bully denizens, who will be preying on people just like you.

Using the opposite, lightweight approach will give you a better mental condition of feeling stronger and faster and will put more oomph in your step. It will help to keep you moving faster and for longer – you can cover more ground like this, which is possibly one of the most important goals. Putting distance between yourself, and danger as fast as possible is imperative.

As a Citizen Survivor, you should have a Plan B, Plan C, Plan D etc. The same thought process should be applied to preparing your bag for survival. So think of it in stages.

Your actual Citizen Survivor bag is just one stage of the whole bug out procedure. It will, no doubt, be the heaviest and bulkiest stage of your preparation.

You should also use a 'belt base' system of pouches as your second stage. This belt should contain only your very essential survival gear (first aid, knife, fire lighting, water filtration, snares and fishing kit etc.).

The final backup, a container based stage should be kept perhaps in a secret area you've previously passed if you need to U-turn for any reason.

By using a system of bug out stages you are then able to prioritise the essential items over the 'nice to have' items. All your essentials should go into your main bindle with your back up survival equipment going into your belt pouches – a typical example would be your survival tin, knife, etc. in the lighter, more mobile belt pack. This method will give you the options to ditch equipment if you were forced to, or to stop and cache the container along the way. If you fear for your supplies and your life, then ditching your main bindle will mean a faster getaway while keeping your essential survival belt and hidden base supplies and equipment.

There is also a fourth stage to consider – a body stage. Typically, this would be a boot knife, compass, torch, survival blanket etc. These items can be carried on your person if needed.

In conclusion – by using this method of preparing your Citizen Survivor supplies, you now have options that cover situations if you were to be accosted and forced to give up your equipment and supplies.

Moaning Minnies
[Omitted by order of the MOS]

Excerpt from the MOS sponsored radio show 'The Adventures of Jack Jones'.

Narrator:
Ladies and gentleman, the adventures of Jack Jones (title music; audience applause). Jack is scrumping on the outskirts of a town and can hear a woman sobbing in her back garden. He leans over the fence to see what all the brouhaha is about.

Jack:
Whatcha' guv (audience laughter)

Woman:
Heavens above, they've taken everything

Jack:
Who have?

Woman:
My neighbours, the Fletcher family, they used to be so lovely. They've just come in and taken it all. My water, my food, my clothes, my bedding. All I've

got left is the clothes on my back.

Jack:
Blimey! I'd rather have a cup of tea to start my day! (Audience laughter) 'Ere, you weren't still chatting to them, were you?

Woman:
Of course, they were my friends, I told them I'd been lucky enough to get together quite a stockpile – and now it's all gone.

Jack:
Bloomin' eck woman (audience laughter), you should never tell anyone what you do or don't have, where you're based, or how many there are in your group. Careless talk costs lives, don't you know!

Woman:
Whatever will I do now?

Jack:
Where's your other half?

Woman:
He went looking for supplies a few weeks ago at the warehouses, and never came back.

Jack:
Blimey! A woman on her own? You've got about as much luck as my old man on the horses (audience laughter). Here, have a read of this handbook from the Ministry

of Survivors (audience applause), that'll tell you all you need to know.

Woman:
Could I come with you? I've got no one left.

Jack:
'Ere I'm Jack Jones, I travel alone, don't you know. You can keep the book for your troubles though. It'll keep you going if you stop thinking like a bloomin' woman (audience laughter).

Woman:
What a prize idiot I've been. I'd be brown bread without you!

Jack:
If you were brown bread I'd butter you myself (audience laughter). Speaking of which, I better scarper before more of your neighbours turn up!

Woman:
Thank you Jack Jones

Jack:
Whatcha'! (Audience applause)

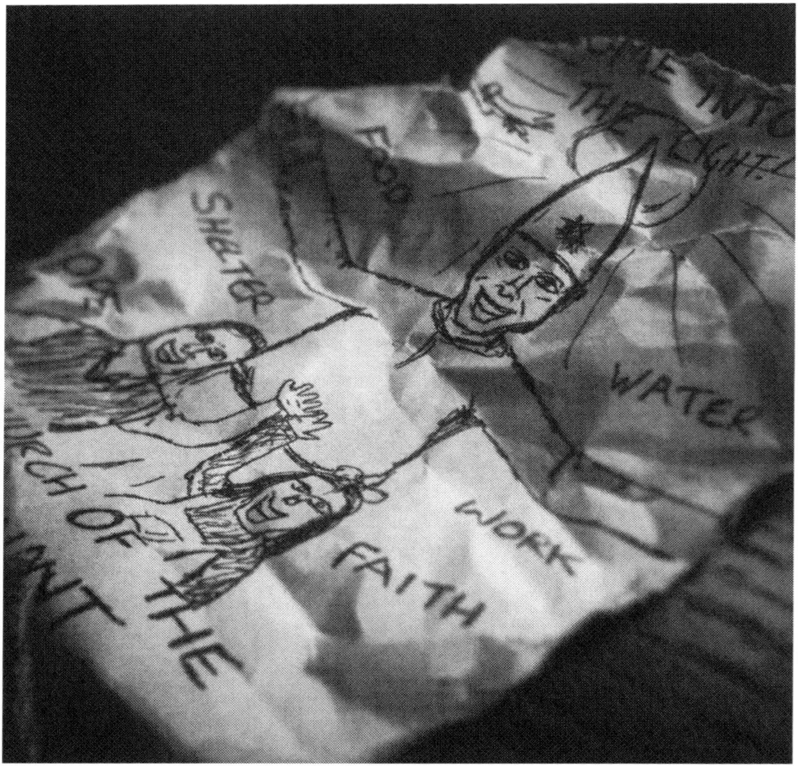

SHELTER
FOOD
WATER
WORK
FAITH

SHELTER

"The wicked are overthrown and are no more, but the house of the righteous will stand."
– Proverbs 12:7; Church of the Remnant

Helter-skelter

Well Citizen Survivor, I expect you're in a bit of a pickle at the moment? Is your stomach rumbling? Are you thirsty? Well, these things must be dealt with, but it's all for nothing unless you've got a roof over your head!

Remember the rule of threes, three weeks with no food, three days with no water, three minutes with no shelter (in extreme weather of course).

In just about any survival situation or any emergency scenario, assuming you are not injured in any way and where you are forced to fend for yourself, then your number one priority is to ensure you can make a good shelter suitable to keep you out of the elements and as safe as you possibly can be. Fortunately, we have relatively few beasties that can do you serious harm in Blighty – no lions or tigers, or bears; oh my! – so we are quite safe out in the wild. Unless you have a fear of hordes of marauding bunnies attacking you, then you're pretty safe here in the good old British Isles, from animals at least.

The bad luck, on the other hand is the fact that we do not have the huge expanses of pure wilderness and terrain that's suitable for 'just disappearing' like our lucky cousins over in the US of A and many other countries.

As we have touched on previously, bugging out is to move on, to leave a fixed base and head out for pastures new. An ideal environment would be an abandoned country house, away from main roads and prying eyes, but you've got to get there first. Just a thought though, remember – these buildings are abandoned for a reason! If you're lucky, it was simply a case that the past occupier wasn't capable of surviving and died of thirst or hunger with no other nasty business.

Now you've left those townies behind, let's get a roof over your head Citizen Survivor!

Emergency Community Shelters (ECP)
[Removed from this edition of the handbook as no longer relevant.]

When hell freezes over
It can be hard for the novice Citizen Survivor to get his head round the fact that shelter is more important than food and water, particularly if they've spent their previous life in a brick house, but let's explore this a bit further.

The MOS do not particularly recommend being on

the move in the winter months but we must remain pragmatic and understand that water, food and safety are other considerations.

Let's think about hypothermia. Hypothermia is the result of your core body temperature dropping below what is required for normal functions and metabolism. Typically, a drop of three degrees in your core temperature means you have hypothermia. On average, normal body temperatures are between 98-100°F (36.5 and 37.5°C). You do not have to be exposed to extreme cold for hypothermia to be at risk.

If you are exposed to temperatures around 50°F, (10°C), and have on wet clothing or are submerged in water then hypothermia is a serious threat. What are you doing in the bloomin' water anyway? Being exposed to what you would consider cool temperatures for prolonged periods without protection can bring on hypothermia as well. Older adults and younger children are particularly at risk.

Outside your shelter

The winter months can be deadly for people if they do not protect themselves. Your clothing is the first line of defence against the cold. Clothing should be layered with material such as wool or fleece next to the skin. Cotton is not a material you want next to your skin because it will hold body moisture (sweat) next to the skin.

The process of evaporation of sweat is what cools the body and you will sweat even in cold weather on exertion. You want material that wicks the moisture away from the skin to reduce the evaporative process.

The next layer can be the last layer if it is insulated and waterproof otherwise you will need an additional outer layer that is wind and waterproof.

Layering of clothing allows you to regulate your body temperature to reduce sweating. If you feel warm, you can remove a layer to cool down slightly. Once cooled put the layer back on to prevent chilling. You must do what you can to prevent heavy sweating and thus body cooling in cold temperatures. It will only take minutes in some cases to develop signs of hypothermia.

The neck, head, armpits and groin area must be covered at all times when exposed to the cold. Large arteries in these areas carry blood to and from the organs and warm blood flows from your inner core to the surface to warm the extremities and if these areas are exposed, the blood will cool faster than the body can warm up.

Warm air always conducts to extreme cold air so if your head is exposed the warm body heat will conduct away from the body. It is important that you have protection that reflects body heat back to the body and not away from the body. Thermal blankets are ideal for protection from the cold because they are designed in some cases to reflect over 90 percent of body heat back to the body.

Inside your shelter
If you are inside an abandoned home, you should gather everyone in one room in the centre of the home.

Plan to have them sleep there if it is possible. If there are windows or doors that lead outside, you should cover them from the inside with thermal blankets or other material to keep heat from conducting to the extreme cold outside. The warmer it is inside the home the faster heat will conduct to the outside and this is an endless process; don't use your valuable heat trying to warm up the Universe!

Insulation between you and the floor is important when you are sleeping. If you are on a slab, body heat will conduct into the cooler surface and if you have subfloors, heat will conduct through the floor into the cooler space under the home. An emergency sleeping mat is ideal to prevent this, giving both thermal and reflective insulation between your body and the floor.

Remove as much clothing as possible when sleeping if you have adequate blankets or sleeping bags. Clothing (including socks) will get damp from perspiration and can cause body cooling if left next to the skin when sleeping. It is particularly important that you do not sleep with wet/damp socks on.

The digestive process will raise the body's core temperature, so have everyone eat before sleeping to help warm the body overnight when it is the coldest.

Be mindful of staying in abandoned homes too long though; the owners may return. If not, the bully denizens will soon be investigating.

If you are stranded without shelter

If there is not a shelter immediately available, you must get out of the extreme cold and begin working on a makeshift shelter. Getting under pine trees with heavy evergreen boughs can break the wind and it makes it easier to construct a shelter out of ponchos, tarps, branches or thermal blankets.

If there is deep snow on the ground, you can excavate the snow and create four walls of snow to break the wind. Dig down to bare ground if possible. If you have tarps or ponchos, use them for overhead cover. Leave enough space in the cover for smoke to escape if you have the means to build a fire. Ensure you have ground insulation such as pine needles, other vegetation or thermal blankets. Do not lean against the walls of snow; this will prevent heat loss. The snow cave or shelter must be large enough for you to lie down without touching the sides. Properly constructed snow shelters can be as much as 15 degrees warmer than the outside air.

Try to get yourself off the ground if possible. If your shelter is fully enclosed then the higher up in your shelter the better. Any heat that accumulates will be at the top. If it is fully enclosed, make sure you have a fresh air flow high up.

Ideally, as a Citizen Survivor, it's worth considering carrying a storm shelter if venturing out in possible snow and blizzard conditions.

Emergency evacuation

You may be put in a situation where you have to evacuate on foot and carry your emergency essentials with you. An emergency evacuation in simple terms means you are leaving a dangerous situation for one less dangerous. Having to make this choice in cold temperatures has its own unique set of challenges.

Exertion will cause sweating, which in turn cools the body. Layering of clothing is very important if you are hiking. You will have to take periodic breaks to allow your body to cool. Having dry socks available at all times is crucial and you should always have an adequate supply with you. You can develop trench foot (sometimes referred to as immersion foot) from having wet feet for prolonged periods, and especially when exposed to cold temperatures. However, it does not have to be below freezing for you to develop trench foot. Wet feet will also mean a colder body. Dry your socks over a fire if possible and if not over a fire, open air dry and warm in a coat pocket before putting back on.

Make sure you shoes/boots are fully waterproof first (scrump a good pair of hiking boots as soon as possible). Don't let any water get into your footwear if you can avoid it. If not, stuff your feet into plastic bags first before putting your footwear on.

Your bindle should have shelter materials and we assume you would have cold weather gear on. It is important that you have adequate clothing so you can change out of damp clothes into dry warm ones. Always dry any article of clothing thoroughly before putting back into your pack.
Ensure your pack is protected from moisture such as

rain or snow by having a poncho large enough to cover you and your pack. A wet pack on your pack will cause your body heat to conduct to the cold wet pack.

When taking a break check your feet, fingers, ears and cheeks for frost bite. The skin may feel numb and be slightly lighter in colour to the point of whiteness, which means blistering is not far off. Blisters filled with clear fluids indicate mild frostbite; blood or cloudy liquid indicates severe frostbite.

To treat mild frostbite warm the body part immediately by gently blowing on it, placing under your armpits if physically possible or cupping with your hands if it is an ear lobe. Cover or otherwise protect the area once warmed to prevent irritation from friction.

Treatment for severe frostbite is a bugger, we're afraid you've most likely had it if you suffer from this, unless there is some miracle. If you still have any fight in you, warm the affected area slowly and cover once warmed. There will be pain associated with severe frostbite as the affected part warms.

Extreme cold is a killer and regardless of how long you expect to be exposed, you should be properly dressed for the cold. Hypothermia, if left untreated, is fatal and severe frostbite left untreated will result in the loss of limb and/or tissue, and can lead to gangrene which is fatal if left untreated. Basically, you're brown bread!

Remember Citizen Survivor – Nothing separates the men from the boys like winter, so be prepared!

Hyperthermia

Although it's unlikely to be much of an issue in Blighty, it would be remiss of us not to include information on hypothermia's deviant cousin, hyperthermia.

Prevention must be part of your Citizen Survivor skills and when it comes to heat exhaustion it is vital to know the heat stroke symptoms before the onset of full blown heatstroke, also known as hyperthermia. In some cases it may not be possible to prepare properly so it is important to know how to protect yourself using what is available in the wild.

Knowing what the morbid outcome can be goes a long way to preventing certain situations from happening in the first place. Forget what your old man told you, heat stroke and dehydration are not the same things. Heatstroke happens when the body fails to maintain its own cooling functions due to any excessive exposure to higher temperatures.

Dehydration is simpler; your body does not have enough fluids for normal cell and organs function. This is fatal; the body only has to lose 12-18% of its fluids. Let's not get bogged down in all this again, we've said all you need to hear on dehydration.

Do remember though Citizen Survivor – three days without water is all you've got

In some very extreme cases, it may be possible to survive longer than three days, but it would essentially mean that you do not move and why on earth would you want to risk it?

The cooling process takes place when you begin to sweat and the moisture on your skin then starts to evaporate, cooling the skin first, and then ultimately the blood in capillaries, veins and arteries that are close to the surface. The warm blood flows from the various organs to the surface of the skin, causing it to be cooled and the blood then travels back to the organs to lower their temperature.

A simple method to keep the body cool is by simply wetting your clothing and keeping your head covered with a wet cloth. It is important to conserve sweat and never attempt to ration any water. If you are in the hotter areas of the wild it is important to reduce the amount of sweating – and in order to conserve bodily fluids you should not exert yourself during the hottest parts of the day.

Keep under any shaded areas if possible, as this can help slow the dehydration process and thus help prevent heatstroke. If core body temperatures rises above 40.5°C (105°F) – it must be cooled down immediately or it is fatal.

If you're travelling with others and one of them suffers from heatstroke, whenever possible submerge the patient in water. If this is not possible, cool the head and body with wet cloths, give fluid, lie the victim down and raise the feet.

Typically, as you grow as a journeyman Citizen

Survivor, you will become knowledgeable and aware of heat stroke symptoms and dehydration signs, as well as the actual risk of heatstroke during your adventures.

Planning your day is essential, as is ensuring you have the correct equipment with you – correct clothing and head wear must be worn and your day planned in such a way as to ensure you do not overwork yourself and thus overheat.

- Heat stroke can only be induced by exposure to heat. Therefore, if you are in the wild, plan your route so as to travel during the cooler parts of the day and rest up when it is very hot.
- Rest frequently – you burn a huge amount of energy when it hot – take your time. Avoid dehydration by drinking little and often – never skip a drink – if you feel thirsty, chances are you are already starting to dehydrate.
- Set intervals where you can rest up under shade where possible and allow your body to cool off
- Keep out of the sun's heat.
- If there is no natural shade, make some, you wally; improvise. Use a blanket draped over a tree branch.

Tarp
When scrumping, there are few things more valuable and precious then good old tarp. Never overlook how useful tarp is, and you should stock as much of this as possible and certainly always carry some with you. An ideal scenario would be to secure your tarp to the top of a downed tree and slant to the

ground on the north side in cold weather. Secure it with wooden stakes or rocks.

When it comes to tarps, be mindful of the quality and watch out for tears and damage. You will definitely regret a ripped one in the middle of the night when it's windy and raining! A quality tarp will ensure a dry night's sleep and if you've secured it well enough it will stay put if there's any wind as well. Quite often it's a good idea to use short straps to secure your tarp rather than rope or para-cord. This will ensure a bit of movement in windy condition and prevent any extra force on your tarp. An ordinary tarp is ideal for emergency survival shelters and can be set up in a matter of minutes using what you find in your environment.

Once constructed, use whatever is available to provide additional insulation. If you carry tarps in your pack (and we hope for your sake you do!), we recommend they have grommets so you can secure with rope or combine tarps together to make a larger shelter.

If you do not have a tarp, you can slant saplings or a thermal blanket and vegetation to create a windbreak and to provide overhead cover. Build your fire so the heat is reflected into the makeshift shelter (more on fire later). Fill in with vegetation to leave just enough room to enter. If the ground is flat, excavate the soil to provide a depression that will fit your body.

If the situation allows, always pick tarp that is camouflaged or earth toned, a garish and colourful tarp will have you sticking out like a sore thumb, not good news if there are any dubious chaps about! Keep your emergency tarp shelter as low to the ground as possible – it will help protect it from wind, keep it compact, there will be less area to heat up and it will reduce the silhouette outline.

Thermal blankets

A survival shelter can also be constructed using thermal blankets. These are easily packed and you should always have at least six in your pack. You can use them as ground insulation, as well. You have to use caution with fire near the thermal blankets yet you want the heat to reflect inside the structure.

Build a fire at the opening and set up a reflector behind the fire so the heat is directed toward the opening. You can put a series of stakes in the ground and pile up green vegetation to direct the heat toward the opening.

Building a survival shelter is the most important thing you can do if you find yourself stranded in the wilderness. A shelter will make the difference between surviving and ending up six feet under and you will find you can survive extremely harsh conditions if you have protection from the elements. Wandering around looking for help will only slow down you down, and even if you came across someone, there is no guarantee they would help you. Stay in place, and set up camp; tomorrow is another day.

Concealing your camp

You don't need to be a penny short of a bob to know that it's in your interest that your camp is as concealed as possible.

The MOS used to train soldiers in SERE (Survival, Evasion, Resistance and Escape). The philosophy of those that had been through the training was that if you can master 'Survival and Evasion' you do not need to worry about 'Resistance and Escape'. Don't worry too much about all that. In other words, learn how to survive and evade others in the wilderness so you are not caught with your trousers down.

Camouflage

Blend in with your environment by changing the way things appear to the human eye. Shiny metal or glass objects are not natural in the wild so they have to be subdued. Your outline and the outline of your shelter and equipment must be changed so it does not obviously look like a tent or other forms of shelter. Your shelter should not be an unnaturally bright colour or have any highly visible ropes or poles. If you're in the wild, a scrumped camouflage tent would be ideal to avoid obvious detection. However, you're very lucky if you've got one of these, so the rest of you must still break up the outlines by using materials natural to the area.

However, ripping out bushes, and cutting limbs to cover a tent can leave an obvious trail into your camp area – so you have to be able to camouflage without leaving a footprint. Vegetation, once cut, will turn brown over time, so if you expect to be in the area for an extended time you want to avoid having dead vegetation lying about covering things, because this is a giveaway for anyone in the know who may be sniffing about.

Take small amounts of vegetation from one area, move to another, and then use the materials a distance away from your shelter or camp.

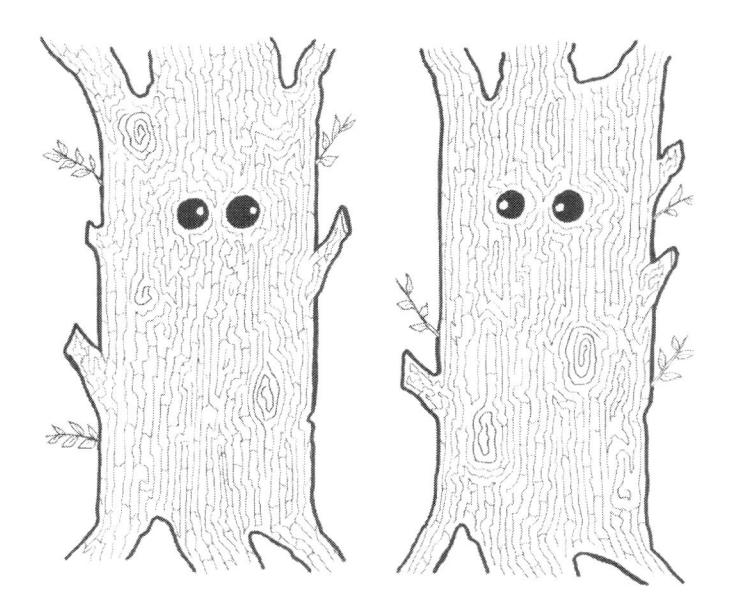

Cover and concealment

Many Citizen Survivors get these two things confused and assume they mean the same thing. Cover is protection from direct or indirect hostilities whereas concealment means you are hidden visually to avoid detection and does not necessarily mean you are protected from hostilities.

Natural shades and colour

Certain colours are natural to nature and the human eye will pass over colours when scanning if they belong in the environment. Browns, forest greens, and even certain coloured flowers are to be expected in woodland areas. However, bright oranges, blues and certain other colours are easily detected because the brain immediately realizes they do not belong. You can use mud, sticks and leaves as a means of concealing yourself and equipment.

In forested areas, blotches work best because of how the sunlight dapples the forest floor during the day. Solid colours would stand out, so dab mud, sticks and leaves in various places. Fill in the gaps with other materials found in the area such as green foliage from conifers to achieve the blotchy look. Keeping your camp height below any bushes or foliage height will conceal you whereabouts quite nicely too.

The human body

Instinctively humans are programmed to recognize faces and will always fix on any object that appears to have a face and people even imagine faces in the clouds. Have a look next time you walk past an abandoned two up, two down with a door in the middle and you'll see what we mean.

You have to break up your face and to cover shiny skin – mud is a favourite, along with weaving sticks and vegetation in your hair or headgear. This breaks up the shape of the human head and face. Humans and most animals immediately recognize the silhouette/shape of the human body as it is standing and moving, so it must be broken up so it is not easily recognized.

Fast movement attracts attention, and experienced folk know never to stare directly at anything. They catch movement out of the corner of their eyes and this is especially true in low light conditions. Do not climb over objects such as downed trees or over large boulders. Your silhouette is exposed. Never walk up right over the crest of a hill or over any high spot in the terrain for the same reason. When walking upright such as when stalking game or eluding other humans, take half steps and feel what is under your feet before putting your weight down, a turned rock or snapping twig can reveal your location.

Anyone that has been in the wild for any period soon realizes that the nose becomes more tuned to the smell of the natural surroundings, and scents not normal to the environment can easily be detected – this includes human scent. Tobacco smoke can be detected by the human nose from several miles away in some cases, not a problem now though unless you've scrumped a tobacconist! If you've scrumped colognes or other unnatural scents, use your loaf and get rid of them now. Smoke your clothes and body with hardwoods from the area, apply fresh mud to your clothes, and body if you need to mask odours while hunting game.

Obviously, anything that rattles on your body will make noise so it must be secured.

MINISTRY OF SURVIVORS

Excerpt from the MOS sponsored radio show 'The Adventures of Jack Jones'.

Narrator:
Ladies and gentleman, the adventures of Jack Jones (title music; audience applause). Jack is scrumping in the woods and comes across a lone fellow collecting grey water from a stream.

Jack:
Whatcha' guv (audience laughter).

Arthur:
Hello boss, lovely day for it.

Jack:
Lovely day for it? Blimey, I've not even had a sniff of it since the missus went doolally (audience laughter).

Arthur:
To who do I have the pleasure of making acquaintance?

Jack:

Jack Jones squire, you?

Arthur:
Arthur.

Narrator:
Jack notices that Arthur has no filtering equipment with him (audience laughter).

Jack:
'Ere, I hope you're not going to have that?

Arthur:
Have what?

Jack:
The fisherman's daughter.

Arthur:
I'll do no such thing, I don't even know her! (Audience laughter)

Jack:
No you bloomin' idiot, the water! You've got no filtering gear.

Arthur:
But this is running water Jack, you don't need to filter running water.

Jack:
Don't need to? Don't need to! Blimey Arthur, Arthur mind more like (audience laughter). If you drink grey water you've had it. Here have a read of this handbook

from the Ministry of Survivors (audience applause), that'll tell you all you need to know.

Arthur:
Ministry of Survivors?

Jack:
The gaffers upstairs, you nincompoop! (Audience laughter).

Arthur:
Well, thank you Jack. What a prize idiot I've been. I'd be brown bread without you!

Jack:
If you were brown bread I'd butter you myself (audience laughter). Speaking of which, I'm peckish, off I go.

Arthur:
Thank you, Jack Jones.

Jack:
Whatcha'! (Audience applause).

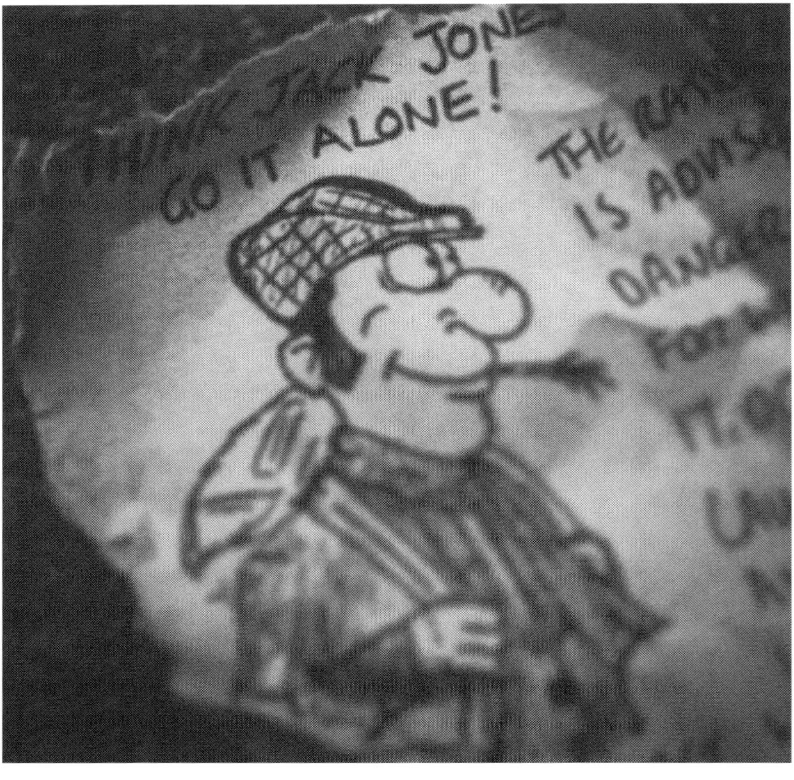
GO IT ALONE!

WATER

"Drink water from your own cistern, running water from your own well." – Proverbs 5:15; Church of the Remnant

Water, water everywhere and not a drop to drink?
You may think that because you are miles from civilisation that any water source would be safe to drink but this is simply not the case. After obtaining shelter, water is your next priority and regardless of your current supply, you should begin immediately securing a source. In most cases, you will have to filter and purify any surface water source you find. Always assume surface water sources are contaminated by animal faeces, carcases and by countless human mischiefs as well.

The water source will contain harmful bacteria, parasites and pathogens that will cause illness or worse. The water must be filtered and purified before it would be considered safe to drink. Acceptable methods of water purification include: chemical treatment using iodine or chlorine dioxide tablets, or sodium hypochlorite (liquid chlorine); by boiling and filtering the water; or by using a portable water filtration system. As always, and not to bang the drum, let's wean you off the old ways and concentrate on boiling and filtering.

If you are currently without water, why not make a note on a calendar that you and your loved ones will be dead in three days as a reminder for you to pull your socks up!

Dehydration
Dehydration is a nasty old business, and something to avoid at all costs. A good idea is to observe the colour of your urine, if it's clear – do not fear, if it's brown, get some water down. Essentially the darker your urine is, the more dehydrated you are.

We will not list all of the signs and symptoms of dehydration, as we have already discussed this. It would be an exercise in sadism and we expect you are aware if you're not drinking enough, but here are a few reminders;
- Severe headaches
- Lethargy
- Constipation
- Seizures
- Delirium
- Nausea
- Painful passing of urine
- Death

Nasty old business indeed. Now we've glanced over that one, let's get you a drink!

Water myths

There are many drinking water myths and old wives' tales about finding and drinking water.

By following this nonsense you could easily land up in a worse condition than when you started; it will probably lead to severe illness and even death. Still, that means more drinking water for the rest of us with our heads screwed on!

Below are a few common myths about how, when and where you can drink water.

Eat some snow to rehydrate you

When you consider that snow is ice cold, it then makes sense that it will require lots of energy calories to warm it for proper digestion when in your stomach. By eating ice cold snow, you are cooling your core body temperature – this can lead to hypothermia. As snow lays on the ground it will collect a lot of different types of bacteria and other organisms – this bacteria and organisms can easily make you ill. Always melt snow or ice before ingesting and definitely stay away from snow that is discoloured, e.g. yellow snow, yes – it's yellow for a reason! If you melt snow first it can then be boiled and purified.

Drink salt water when desperate

NO, never drink sea water! Sea water will increase your body's dehydration level and you'll be a goner in no time. In fact, drinking sea water will cause death even faster than having nothing to drink in the first place. In excessive heat, you can use salt water to help cool your body down (bathing, splashing it on your neck etc.), but never drink it.

If it's from a stream or running river water, it's safe to drink

This is rarely true … on the odd occasion a fresh glacier stream may be clean but not always. Remember, you don't know where that stream has been before you met it! You have no idea what it passed over or what it came in contact with along its merry path to you either. There could be animal waste, even dead birds, large animals or citizens more ignorant than you lying in the upstream. Essentially, if you have to make a choice between still or running water, the running water has less chance of being contaminated – but always try to filter the water, even if it's just through a cloth or bandana, anything will help to try and purify it a bit more.

You can drink your own urine

Technically it's a yes, BUT very, very small amounts and you won't make any friends among your fellow Citizen Survivors for doing it. Remember, urine contains all your body's toxins – of which most are extremely toxic and considered dangerous to your body in the first place, that's why the body has chucked them out. Even small amounts should only be considered in the most extreme circumstances. Urine will not rehydrate you – you are only using the body's waste to try and rehydrate, by doing this it will slow your natural functions and this process actually uses more body fluid to process! Remember – if you are thirsty, it's your body's way of telling you, you are already dehydrated.

Drinking from a puddle or pond or dip in the road is fine
Of course you shouldn't drink from a pond or puddle, who do you think you are, a Labrador? The same rules apply here as with all of the above. You have no idea what's been in that water before you – it could even be a sewage run off! Always stop and think first before drinking from an unknown water source – and definitely treat and purify the water first. Now we've got that mumbo-jumbo out of the way, it's time to get ready to drink!

Rain water

Collecting and using rain water can be a great way to conserve resources at home and in your situation it may well be your only choice for drinking water. However, rainwater is not quite as pure and clean as you may might think, so never assume the rain dripping down is safe to drink. Even as the rain pours down it has collected many airborne particles and contaminates.

Let's assume you're in a house. As the rain pours down and off your roof it has a happy time soaking up anything that just happens to be on your roof. Typically, any form of waste or bird poo will wash down from your roof and then easily be absorbed into any rainwater that passes it. So if you're trying to collect it, you can guarantee it's already contaminated with something that can cause you problems. Bacteria, viruses, parasites and numerous chemicals can also be carried along in rain water – all of these can lead to an upset stomach at best and severe disease at worse.

There are, however, a few things that can make your rain water better or worse, namely your location and how you store that water. Also the temperature the water is stored at.

Whatever collection method you use the water will not be anywhere near clean enough or safe enough to drink – in a nutshell, stored water from collected rain water should only ever be used for watering plants!

From a Citizen Survivor perspective you would

most likely be collecting rain water for drinking and cooking purposes only. So for the purpose of cooking you will be boiling the water, making it safe to cook with. However, collected water for drinking must be safe to drink.

So the answer to the question of 'can you drink rain water' is generally a big no, but, with the right equipment you definitely can drink rain water, pond water, river water. You just filter it properly first.

Now we'll get to how to do that.

Community Water Collection Points (CWCP)
[Removed from this edition of the handbook as no longer relevant.]

Collect, filter, boil, store, repeat

Harvesting 'grey water'
'Grey Water' is water you can't drink, but don't concern yourself with that yet, just get as much 'grey water' as you can! It doesn't matter whether you're a townie, out on the trail, in the wilderness, by the coast, or anywhere else for that matter, you will still need fresh drinking water, and you'll need it now!

One of the simplest yet most effective rain water harvesting methods you could ever think of, is to simply use a stretched out tarp or some old guttering or pipes to harvest any rain water. Set up old guttering or pipes close to your camp or where you've hunkered down, and use them to collect the rain. A top tip is to set them up in trees and bushes as the leaves and foliage will help to allow even more rain down your guttering system. From here just angle the pipes into a storage container of some sort, perhaps a water butt or an old oil drum and hey presto, that wasn't so hard was it?

Being able to capture your rain water easily is essential. A pre filter is also a good idea to have 'in-line' that intercepts any large debris or dead critters! You will still have to treat the water to get safe, drinkable water, but by adding the pre filter you can at least get rid of some of the big stuff.

It goes without saying some good filtration will be needed after collection in order to ensure clean, safe drinking water, but for 'grey water' usage this method is perfectly fine. You've got the water, we'll tell you how to clean it later. If you really find yourself away from civilisation and lacking resources, sometimes you may find yourself in a situation in which you will need to make do with whichever resources you can find. In these events, basic storage and collection devices such as empty bottles or containers will work just fine and can actually provide you with a selection of pretty effective rain water harvesting methods.

If you are looking to use empty plastic bottles to store your water, it's recommended that you use a knife or sharp implement, and remove the narrow top of the bottle to help open it up and increase the storage capacity. By doing this, you make the opening larger and therefore allow more rain water to make its way inside. If you have, or can find, multiple bottles or similar containers, set them up strategically and use leaves and foliage as a form of guttering system to allow more rain inside. The more you set up, the more rain water you'll be able to harvest.

If you are harvesting rain water in this way, make sure that you secure your bottles firmly into the ground as the last thing you want is them falling over when they get too full, stolen by a desperate neighbour or being knocked over by animals perhaps. Try digging a shallow hole and half burying the bottle and then firmly packing the soil around the edges to help hold your bottles firmly in place.

To get the most from any type of rain collection method you have to try and catch as much rain as possible. Just about anything will do - a tarp, sheet, raincoat, groundsheet, bin liner, plastic bag... Anything to give a larger catchment area. So, by using as big a catchment area as you can find and then funnelling that rain water towards your containers will give very fast results. A 2,000 sq. ft. roof is only 20' x 100', (6m x 30m) and if you have a pitched roof with two sides, it only has to be 20' x 50' (3m x 15m). With only 1" (25mm) of rain you're going to be able to collect 1,250 gallons of water - that's over 5500 litres!

If you have a house with no gutters to direct the rainfall, there are different rain water harvesting methods that will work just as well. Building your own system is one of them.

Finding water

As a Citizen Survivor, you will soon learn how to purify water (or die trying!) but before you can get started, you have to find water first. MOS guidelines suggest you ween yourself off scavenging purification tablets and bottled water as soon as possible, you are only delaying the inevitable! The simplest suggestion is to have a site near to a river, stream or lake. However, other survivors will have the same idea so you must make this judgement based on your current situation; running water is always preferable over stagnant water.

You may not always have such a water source near your site – in fact you may have to dig for it or collect it using other methods that will be described but first how to dig for water. Dry wash or shallow gullies can be a source of water, particularly if there is green vegetation along the sides. These washes usually have water flowing at various times. In the dryer seasons, the flow diminishes or stops completely but there can be water just below the surface.

Keep an eye out for green vegetation in any dry environment. The plant life could not survive on the rock outcropping unless there was a water source just below the surface. You may find a natural spring is seeping through a fissure in the rocks and is filling up a small cistern. In years past people constructed cisterns to collect spring water; pooled water is easier to collect. Any water collected from a cistern must be purified; animals will use the source as well and will have contaminated it. If you find such a source, tell no one and keep it under your hat. You don't want a gang of bully denizens setting up shop next to you!

Remember Citizen Survivor – If you don't have access to water, keep moving, you oughta!

Basic layer filter

Not only must you know how to purify water, Citizen Survivor, you must also learn how to filter it properly first. Water must be filtered to remove waterborne cysts that can harbour and protect bacteria from chemical treatment or even boiling. The cysts can be described as micro sized seedpods that can withstand high temperatures. Filtering will remove these cysts along with pesticides, herbicides, sediment, insects and other debris.

Filtering mediums include charcoal, sand, gravel and cloth. Layer the filtering mediums with the finer material as the bottom layer to filter out the microorganisms. Use any tin food can with a hole in the bottom, plastic bottle or any other suitable container that did not contain chemicals or other toxins. Plastic bottles are preferred by MOS so we recommend you collect as many of these when scrumping as possible.

This is a slow process so have as many filters in operation as your situation allows. You have to get this right, Citizen Survivor and get it into your thick skulls, because filtering really is the difference between life and death!

1. Have at least two containers, one for grey water, and one for filtered water

2. If you are using a bottle, cut the bottom of the bottle off. Take off the lid and cover it with cloth using a rubber band or anything else to hand. This is where your water will filter out from. If not, make very small holes in your grey water filter, enough for the water to pour out slowly, but not for the filtering materials to escape.

3. Gather your filtering materials; small rocks, gravel, sand and grass for example.

4. Crush charcoal from your campfire into very small pieces.

5. Arrange materials to create a decent filter. Arrange your layers to filter larger pieces out first, then smaller ones. A properly layered filter would be gravel or rocks at the top, sand and charcoal in the middle and sand at the bottom to catch the smallest particles (obviously this means you'll put the sand in first).

6. Place your filter with the holes at the bottom into your filter water container.

7. Place a cloth or bandana over the large opening at the top to act as a first layer if possible.

8. Pour the grey water through your filter; if time is not an issue, it wouldn't hurt to do this one more than once.

9. Well done, got this far? You should now have a container of filtered water. DON'T DRINK IT YET! You need to boil it first.

There are many variations to filtering water, which we are confident you'll pick up on your travels, you can eventually do this with all natural materials, but you're not Tarzan, Johnny Weissmuller! So stick with the above for now.

Boiling

Your filtered water looks good, right? Wrong! Grey water that has been filtered and not boiled is useless; grey water that has been boiled and not filtered is useless too – you must do both. Making fire will be discussed later, but for now let's assume you can make one.

Once the water has passed through the filter, pour it into a metal vessel for boiling. Allow the water to rapid boil for one minute if at sea level and if you suspect you are significantly above sea level, boil for three minutes. Water boils at a lower temperature at higher elevations because of the reduced air pressure, thus the extended boil time. When the water has reached a rolling boil, do not boil it any further. Water temperature cannot get any higher than its boiling point no matter how much heat is applied. After you remove the water from the heat source, it will take time for the water to cool down enough for you to be able to drink it. Boiling longer than the recommended times will cause you to lose water volume through evaporation; this can be problematic if you have a limited source.

Voila (as our French Allies used to say), you have taken your first step to staying alive. You have just turned filthy grey water into filtered, boiled and clean (enough) drinking water. It's a miracle! Give yourself a pat on the back, Citizen Survivor.

Transpiration

For the boffins among you, there is also another water collecting technique called transpiration.

Plants lose water vapour through their epidermal pores or their stomata located on their leaves. Plants absorb carbon dioxide and through transpiration exchange that gas for oxygen, which is present in the vapour they lose through their stomata, but let's not worry about the science, you've got a family to keep alive!

Plastic bags, a weight (such as a small stone) for the bag and some string are needed to collect water using this method. The vapour given off by the leaves will condense on the sides of the bag and drip toward the weight placed in the bag. Clear plastic is ideal because it allows the sun's rays to strike the leaves. Essentially you are harnessing the power of the sun to extract the moisture contained in vegetation and leaves. As the vegetation gets warmer, they, in effect 'sweat' out their water content. Which is drinkable.

The process is generally known as a Solar Still. You can use a plastic bag, but make sure there are no rips, tears or holes in it. Add a weight to the bottom. This can be a stone, only make sure you give it a clean first as it will muddy the water you are trying to collect. Then, find a tree branch with a nice bunch of leaves that look green and healthy and put the bag over the leaves branch and tie it to prevent anything entering the bag like an unwanted insect.

And that's it - leave the bag hanging from the branch

and it will slowly collect the moisture in the bottom of the bag as the moisture inside runs down the inside of the bag. A clear plastic bag is preferred as it will allow sunlight to reach the leaves creating more moisture.

Another very similar way is to collect moisture using the sun's rays is to dig a hole in the soil. Put the soil to one side and then place a container in the middle of the hole. Make sure it is very stable and well supported by digging another smaller hole specifically to place the container into, The last thing you want is the container getting unbalanced and falling over with your water inside it! Now find a bunch of green leaves and scatter them inside the hole around the container.

If you intend to stay put and want to make this a permanent addition to your camp – simply add a method of sucking up the water without disturbing your setup – this can be done by putting a length of tubing into the container and running up along the inside of the hole to the outside and burying under the sheet and soil to keep sealed - you can now drink without needing to disturb anything. Now stretch you plastic sheet across the hole allowing it to sag in the middle. You can now use your 'dug out' soil to cover around the edges of the plastic and keep it in place.

Once that's done gently place a stone in the middle to ensure the plastic remains in a saggy position and stops the plastic from flapping around. As the plastic heats up it will create moisture on the inside of the sheet that will run down the inside and drip into your container.

Both very simple and effective methods of collecting water - it won't be huge amounts, but certainly quench your thirst. MOS recommends a combination of filtering and transpiration if your situation allows. Be mindful, though, that bully denizens and desperate Citizen Survivors may see your water collecting devices, out of sight, out of mind!

Learning how to purify water is not complicated and the methods described are relatively easy to accomplish. Water collection certainly separates the (living) men from the (dead) boys! In some cases, you will have to be prepared by having certain materials with you or have the ability to find those materials in your environment.

Scrumping can result in you finding what you need, such as discarded metal cans or other vessels to boil water in and discarded plastic shopping bags that can used to collect water from green vegetation.
Storing water

After three days without water your internal organs begin to shut down and become damaged leading to a very fast death. You could have the swankiest, most secure base for miles but that is useless without good old uncle H_2O.

This makes both short and long term water storage a very high priority for any Citizen Survivor.
When you consider your body is about 75% water, you don't need to be a Billy Boffin to realise that losing

any of that water will soon affect the rest of your body in various ways. In fact as little as a 2% loss in the water surrounding your cells will give a result of some 20% drop in your energy levels. That's how important water is for your body. MOS guidelines say that you should allow an absolute minimum of 3 pints of water per person per day for drinking. If members of your group aren't pulling their weight, that's something to consider!

However, this may not always be enough as there are many additional factors that can affect your need for water.

- Your body weight
- Physical condition and health
- Amount of physical activity each day
- Altitude
- Climatic conditions

Remember that you don't just use water for drinking – add the fact that you will also need water for personal hygiene, cooking, washing clothes, and women's curiosities (if you have females with you) and if you have pets, they need water to survive too (Incidentally, MOS recommends of disposing of all pets immediately except guard dogs, the fewer mouths the better).

So, 3 pints for drinking, needs to be increased considerably. We would say anything up to 2 gallons per person per day need to be stored in order to have enough for all normal tasks as well just drinking water.

Best types of water storage for Citizen Survivors

Surprisingly, many Citizen Survivors continue to inhabit urban areas – so huge amounts of water storage are out of the question for most them! In fact, nothing will lead to a bloody nose (or worse) quicker than townies fighting over water. Without doubt the simplest method is to build up a store of bottled water. Not hundreds of the little 2 pint bottles but the larger and easily manageable 3 pint bottles.

Using this water storage method will make your new life much easier.

Remember Citizen Survivor – you can never have too much water storage!

Rotate your stock and use the water as you would in normal everyday use, starting with the nearest use by date – as you use one bottle, restock with two new ones, they the go at the back of the pile – that way you not only refresh your stock but add to it each time. Water has a surprisingly long shelf life if looked after correctly. Store it in cool and dry conditions - a cellar is the ideal place if it is dry. Temperatures must be constant for best results. Under these conditions bottled water will easily last two years. At a bare minimum keep the water out of any sunlight – sun will cause mould and algae to form inside the bottle. Even after the two year period has ended, treat it like grey water that is still drinkable if filtered and boiled.

A survival situation that exceeds the use by date will mean making the decision as to using older, out of date, bottles – to our way of thinking, providing you have stored them in conditions that will help preserve them, e.g.: cool, constant temperature and dark storage, you will be safe to use for a much longer time.

Once the containers have been used, they can be reused and filled with filtered water and ready to use again. Essential storage methods of your emergency water:

- Store all water in a dry room.
- Store all water away from any direct or indirect sunlight.
- Store water in a cool room.
- Date mark all water and use in rotation to ensure a 1 year store.
- Do not store your water anywhere near fuel products – petrol, diesel etc.
- Check regularly for any signs of leakage.
- Never discuss water with others or how much you have, not even those you consider friends. You never know what they are capable of if their situation deteriorates, careless talk costs lives.
- Most importantly, keep your water out of sight! Nothing is more inviting to a bully denizen than litres of lovely drinking water!

Hopefully by following the MOS guidance above you and your family will be drinking safe water for many years to come! Let's not get complacent though, man cannot survive on water alone!

Remember Citizen Survivor – collect, filter, boil, store, repeat!

Ministry of Survivors

Excerpt from the MOS sponsored radio show 'The Adventures of Jack Jones'.

Narrator:
Ladies and gentleman, the adventures of Jack Jones (title music; audience applause). Jack is scrumping through the woods and comes across a distressed chap by an unlit campfire.

Jack:
Whatcha' guv (audience laughter).

Man:
'Ere how did you find me out?

Jack:
I could see the smoke from your fire yesterday a mile off; it was harder to ignore than Auntie Barbara on 'er second honeymoon (audience laughter).

Man:
Bloomin' eck guv, well that was yesterday. I can't get this perishing fire lit. To top it off, my missus is as

good as done for.

Jack:
Jack Jones 'ere, let's have a look.

Narrator:
Jack notices the unconscious woman lying in the chap's shelter.

Jack:
Well at least your lugholes will get a rest now (audience laughter). Now let's see what's going wrong.

Man:
Thank you, squire.

Jack:
Hold up a ruddy minute. You've got no bowdrill, no knife. You're less prepared then a Chelsea dowager (audience laughter).

Man:
Well I've been using matches, but they've all run out.

Jack:
Matches? Matches? Who do you think you are? You'll be dining in Kensington and catching the 32 to Piccadilly Square next I bet? (Audience laughter). You want to get yourself off that as soon as you can.

Man:
But I don't know how to make a fire.

> Jack:
> Here, have a read of this handbook from the Ministry of Survivors (audience applause), that'll tell you all you need to know.

> Man:
> Well, thank you Jack. What a prize idiot I've been. I'd be brown bread without you!

> Jack:
> If you were brown bread I'd butter you myself (audience laughter). Speaking of which, I've got water to boil, off I go.

> Man:
> Thank you Jack Jones.

> Jack:
> Whatcha'! (Audience applause)

WORTH IT?
moment of joy for a lifetime of
venereal disease,
and hysteria

FIRE

"Each man's work will become evident; for the day will show it because it is to be revealed with fire, and the fire itself will test the quality of each man's work."
– Corinthians 3:13; Church of the Remnant

Let there be light!

First of all Citizen Survivor, let's take a brief moment to see how far you've come. You've escaped the urban tombs, braved the wild, made a shelter and you've purified drinking water. Congratulations to you. However, we expect you're freezing your backside off at the moment? Let's get you some fire.

There have always been a few tried and tested fire starting methods - these methods require a burning ember to actually ignite your fire. To obtain a burning ember means creating one using the friction method. Friction creates heat and heat combined with more friction will produce a glowing hot ember – sufficient to be added to some dry tinder to achieve a flame. The main object has always been to produce a hot burning ember as quickly as possible, and also using as little effort as possible – once you have it, you then a means to ignite your fuel, namely dry tinder, and from there you have the basis of a fire.

This 'friction method' is an old favourite amongst Citizen Survivors and producing fire this way is very rewarding – but, unfortunately, it can also be quite tiring and time consuming as well as taking a lot of practice to perfect. There are literally hundreds of ways to start a fire if you have the time and resources. However, once you find yourself miles from civilisation (if you're lucky) your fire starting material must be readily available and your methods uncomplicated.

Countless Citizen Survivors have literally been left out in the cold because they have found that the matches they had carried all day in their pockets were no good, they would not light. Matches carried in pockets next to your body will absorb perspiration, making them damp. Matches in backpacks exposed to humidity will become useless as well. As always, we strongly recommend weaning yourself off old luxuries such as matches. It's time to cut the apron strings and grow up!

Ask yourself this, you are miles from home, out in the wild; it is cold and it will be dark soon. Will you suffer or do you have the skills to make a fire with what you can forage from your surroundings? Fire starters or combustibles are everywhere – lint in your pocket, thread from your clothing and of course dry tinder made from wood. However, you still need an ignition source.

Remember, you need fire to boil water, so let's get on with it quickly!

A friendly word of caution

Without teaching you to suck eggs, it's important to remind yourself that any fire, of any sort, is a sign of life and activity to man and beast (and those who are both!). While this can hardly be avoided by the journeyman Citizen Survivor, keep it at the back of your noggin. Think of all those poor blighters in the towns who continued to use their fireplaces. With those smoking chimneys, they were essentially pointing themselves out on a map for all and sundry to come and have a nose!

Fire starting methods

Bowdrill

The absolute end goal for a Citizen Survivor is to learn how to make and use a bow drill. Do not despair too much if you can't manage it, but this should be what you're aiming for. A bowdrill has been used for thousands of years to create a fire using friction. This fire starter method may have various designs and materials but the basic concept is the same, create enough friction to cause heat to make an ember. Use shoelaces, cordage from your pack or rope discarded by others that you could scrump from the area.

The concept, of course, is to spin the drill fast enough and long enough to create an ember in the fireboard. Make sure you have dry tinder available so once you have an ember you can move the fireboard to combine the tinder and ember. Some experts may describe catching the ember under the notch in the fireboard using a leaf or piece of bark. Then they describe moving the hot coal on the piece of bark or leaf to the tinder. Moving the ember can cause it to extinguish, you can drop it or the wind blow it away. Move the board away and bring the tinder to the ember.

The wood file

The wood file is a less complicated technique than the bowdrill. However, this method requires much more effort and both pieces of wood must be extremely dry for this procedure to work.

What you'll need to do is carve a V shape into one of the lengths of wood, and then a matching V shape into the second (which is more cone shaped actually). The 'base plate' where you intend to form and collect you hot ember is cut along a length of wood with your knife making a 'vee' shaped groove in the base plate. Using your knife tip, drag the knife along the wood base plate to create the vee shape. By cutting a similar vee shape on the end of a suitable sized stick you can then put the stick vee into the base plate vee, and by running the sick back and forth along the groove you will create friction. From there, with a bit of trial and error and a large dollop of elbow grease, you'll hold one piece still and go hell for leather with the other to create friction.

However, the wood file method has been field tested thousands of times and will work with some patience and attention to detail. Just don't give up like a nancy boy!

Alcohol as a fire starter
[Removed from this edition of the handbook as no longer relevant.]

Knife and flint
Citizen Survivors should always carry a knife and flint with them. If you don't, you should get scrumping as soon as possible. How you've survived this long without a knife is a miracle! A knife blade and flint or a hard stone and steel can be used to create a spark. Actual natural forming flint is the best material to use with steel.

Alternative methods
If you're lucky, you can start a fire using glass. A piece of broken glass or even a pair of glasses can be used to magnify and focus sunlight to ignite dry tinder. For best results, the sun should be directly overhead but this method will work anytime the sun is shining, you simply have to position yourself correctly. You can use any clear glass you can find. The refraction of glass will concentrate the sunlight onto the tinder in the centre and will ignite it.

Although we don't really recommend this, it's possible to use a tin can. It's worth a go if you're in dire straits. Many folks have had success using a tin can bottom as a reflective material to magnify light. The tin can bottom must be polished to a high reflective nature. You cannot use an abrasive material because scratches in the can will reduce the effectiveness. Use any piece of soft cloth to buff the metal to a high shine. Then place dry tinder on the ground and move the can until sunlight is reflecting off the can onto the tinder. This method will take patience and a steady hand but will work.

Keep at it!

Fire starting material is everywhere – as are other materials and methods that can be used as an ignition source; you just have to know what you are looking for.

Practice your fire starting methods in a controlled environment to gain the skill and self-confidence needed to create fire in any environment. It won't be long until you and your loved ones are sat round a fire singing Kumbaya (not too loudly though, you don't know who is out there).

Finding fire-starting materials
Finding dry wood to start a fire can be prove to be a very difficult process sometimes. In the height of summer, wood is plentiful and dry. Trees will shed limbs and the dead wood will be nicely drying off for you. Eventually it will even fall to the ground making it even easier to collect. The bark will easily peel into strips for kindling.

You can even find fire lighting tinder materials right there growing out of trees – the tinder fungus makes starting a fire very easy and is readily available during the summer months. Always use dead wood for your fire – live or green wood will not burn properly and produce smoke. Even if a branch of deadwood is wet, chance are it will still be dry beneath the bark, so strip away the layers to find the dry wood ready to make your kindling.

Regardless of the size of branch, so long as it dry, it will burn. If it's a large branch use your knife and strip (baton) down along the grain to produce smaller and smaller pieces of kindling. Finally, with the driest bits of wood, using your knife again, gently thumb push the blade to cut slivers along the grain to produce a 'feather stick' ideal kindling for starting a fire as it will be so fine and catch easily. The first phase of a fire is essential; you need to ensure that when you apply an ember it will not be wasted and the fire will ignite. To do that you must have dry tinder below your kindling. Newspaper is effective tinder to start a fire, as is cotton wool. However, it is important to remember to wean yourself off items like this that are in scarce supply and won't be being produced anymore.

Remember a fire needs three things to burn: fuel; an ignition source and oxygen. So don't starve your fire of any of these, don't over-stack the fire too soon, let it build up momentum first. Form a little wood stick pyramid over the tinder first to prevent larger sticks from falling down into the fire and stubbing it out due to lack of oxygen. Slowly and surely build a fire up, do not rush it.

Concealing your campfire
Well done for making and maintaining a fire, hopefully you've managed that. We don't want to undo all your good work but do be mindful that fires are a sign of life and although there won't be much more than a nuisance from animals and insects, it may attract bully denizens and that is something you simply don't want to happen. Naughty chaps like moths to a flame, don't bring yourself to their attention. So think about your emergency escape routes; if you suspect you are being watched, move out of the light source. If you think you're in danger, you may want to move on and see what luck you had in the morning. Worst case scenario and all your kit is gone, but at least you weren't there at the time!

Make your fire as hidden as is practical; if you set up

camp in a low valley without trees, for example, you'll be seen from miles around. One of the better ways of concealing a fire is by using a fire pit. Dig a hole between 12-18 inches deep and then dig a ventilation tunnel to feed oxygen to the fire. Build your fire pit under trees heavy with branches and foliage to disperse any smoke. The flames cannot be seen at night if the fire is going in the pit.

Once the pit is built, construct a tripod to hang cooking utensils on or build a cooking rack over the pit using green saplings. Seasoned wood would likely burn up if you used it as a cooking grate.

Maintaining your fire
A surprisingly difficult job at times! In a sentence, to keep a fire going it must have a base of hot coals to maintain it. Just piling on branch after branch will not give you a fire that can keep itself going. Do you really want to get up every hour in the night to redo your fire?

To keep a fire going without any maintenance, especially during the night, is not too difficult. It just requires a bit of planning.
- Start with larger logs, 3-4 inches diameter, close together, 3 foot long.
- Put another layer of logs on top at 90 degrees to the lower logs, again 3 inch diameter.
- Continue building a pyramid, going down in diameter and length and build about 4 or 6 layers like this all 90 degrees to the layer below.
- On top, start your normal fire and work it until it is large and wide enough for you – this may only be a

small fire if needed.

As that small fire burns it will create a base layer of red hot embers that slowly burn down through the remaining layers – it will carry on doing this all night – in fact it's not uncommon for this type of fire to last ten hours.

In effect, you do not have to keep on adding layers of new wood, the fire is self-feeding and will burn away merrily downwards.

This is a basic survival self-feeding fire method for an all-night fire – you will wake up to a pile of hot ember that just require a few bits of kindling. We like to think you've had the common sense to have kept spare kindling dry all night in your shelter, in order to reinstate it as a nice warm fire to cook your breakfast on!

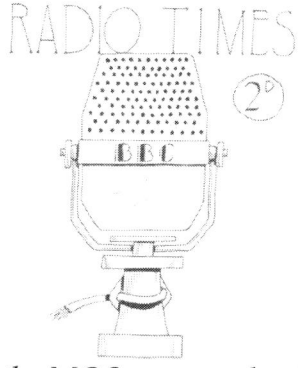

Excerpt from the MOS sponsored radio show 'The Adventures of Jack Jones'.

Narrator:
Ladies and gentleman, the adventures of Jack Jones (title music; audience applause). Jack comes across a young lady watching a rabbit struggle in a snare.

Jack:
Whatcha' guv (audience laughter).

Woman:
Hello my love, I'm Amanda.

Jack:
Jack Jones 'ere, what's all this brouhaha about then?

Amanda:
Oh isn't it awful, look at the poor blighter! All caught up in that snare.

Jack:
Awful? I don't think he put himself in there do you? (Audience laughter) I know

times are tough but I never 'eard of a suicidal rabbit before (audience laughter).

Amanda:
I know Jack, I know, I did it of course. It's just look at its little face, so scared and innocent. I should let it go.

Jack:
I doubt his woodland chums will feel the same about you when their picking at you and you're too weak to fight back because of starvation, you daft 'nana (audience laughter).

Amanda:
Oh Jack, could you do it for me, just this once?

Jack:
Blimey, alright.

Narrator:
Jack takes the rabbit and snaps its neck (sound effect) (audience laughter).

Jack:
There you go darling, get your knickers on and trot along.

Amanda:
Oh Jack, I'm awfully queasy about all this, could you gut it for me too.

Jack:

Who do I look like, bloody Saint Jude (audience laughter). Amanda? Amanda look after ya' more like (audience laughter).

Amanda:
Oh perish the thought!

Jack:
Here have a read of this handbook from the Ministry of Survivors (audience applause), that'll tell you all you need to know.

Amanda:
What a prize idiot I've been. I'd be brown bread without you!

Jack:
If you were brown bread I'd butter you myself (audience laughter). Speaking of which, I better scarper before more of its suicidal rabbit mates turn up and make a right mess of things!

Amanda:
Thank you, Jack Jones.

Jack:
Whatcha'! (Audience applause)

DON'T STOP NOW DARLING
VICTORY!
YOUR OWN FOOD
SELF-SUFFICIENT
A GOOD GIRL

FOOD - IN THE WILD

"For I was hungry and you gave me food, I was thirsty and you gave me drink, I was a stranger and you welcomed me."
– Matthew 25:35; Church of the Remnant

WARNING: If you are really not sure what you are doing, or have any doubts about what you're eating, LEAVE WELL ALONE! Countless people are poisoned (some fatally) from foraging mushrooms alone. Illness is most likely a death sentence in the wild so be vigilant at all times.

If you're in a situation where food is either in short supply or non-existent then you're going to have to fend for yourself. This means ensuring you have the survival skills to live off the land, using your own wits to ensure you don't starve.

You will need your head screwed on to CATCH, KILL, BUTCHER, COOK & PRESERVE any food you can get – and you need to learn those skills now. Was that your stomach rumbling then?

Finding enough food will become your number one daily concern – hunting, trapping and fishing are your best options in the short term; preserving will come next, with growing your own food naturally following later. Ask yourself this question – could I kill an animal – a nice fluffy bunny, hopping around all playful and full of life?

If the answer is no, then in the words of Jack Jones, "You're brown bread", simple as that and, nice as berries are, you're not going to last more than a few weeks. Without doubt, once you have a shelter to call 'home', you have to be on a quest to find food by whatever means you can. That's going to mean using trapping and snares along with a fishing rod, catapult or any other means you can. Also, let's not underestimate the morale boost a warm meal is, soon you'll be feasting like it was Christmas!

Fishing
This is probably the easiest of methods to obtain food. Fish aren't all cuddly like a rabbit, so it's easier for some people to just bash them on the head and that's it – done. Fishing skills are important but you do not need to be a master to catch fish.

In fact, you don't even have to put any real effort into fishing anyway. If you're lucky enough to scrump an automatic reel they will sense the fish, strike the fish and even reel it into shore for you while you're off doing something else.

When you consider that Blighty is an island surrounded by water with many inland rivers and ponds, it makes sense to carry a fishing kit as you'll never be too far away from some water and therefore some fish. It's possible to find a source of good food from many rivers.

Fishing is one of the quickest ways to obtain food in the wild and it can be done with limited skills and materials. Essentially, all you need is line, hooks and bait, or you can catch them by hand or by using a spear.

The main problem is catching the fish in the first place – this is where a good quality fishing kit is required by all Citizen Survivors. It needs to be able to stand up to the job but also be suitably compact and light enough to have in your bag.

Line can be shoelaces, string, clothing torn into strips and braided or you can make cordage by stripping cattail stalks, for example, and twisting the fibres into line.

Hooks can be pieces of wire, paper clips, or bones and pieces of wood carved into hooks.

Use the pop tops off discarded soda cans or even use a broken button as a gorge hook. A gorge hook is sharpened on both ends and is usually about five centimetres long. Both ends are baited with the hopes the fish swallows the entire hook.

Having survival skills means you adapt to your surroundings and know how to use what you find there for your survival.

Remember, you're not out on a jolly, to catch a nice fishy or two then throw them back. Your fishing kit is an essential part of your gear but without all the normal clobber you would expect from a fishing trip from the good old days.

Essentially you can do one of a few things; spear them; hook them or net them.

Traditional fishing methods can be time consuming and require effort that will burn up valuable calories. Therefore, as a Citizen Survivor, it's important to always carry some equipment to ensure you can have food.

Fishing methods
These are the four main choices for survival fishing:

- Hook and line with a hand reel
- Automatic reel, line and hook
- Gill Net & Cast Net Fishing
- Spear fishing

Hook Fishing
When it comes to survival fishing, most people think of the good old hook and line type. This is certainly one of the mainstays of fishing.

But the main idea of a Citizen Survivor fishing kit is something that's light, compact and requires little time to setup and even less to manage.

If you have to spend hours sitting along the river bank watching and waiting for a fish, then that's definitely not practical in your situation and just a waste of your valuable time and effort!

For that reason alone we do not recommend the normal rod and line approach.

Auto reel

The daddy of all fishing techniques is the auto-reel. If you get hold of one of these then you're the cat who got the cream, and you can expect a lot of envious neighbours!

Once set up, the reel is left to work on its own – the mechanism is sensitive to a fish nibbling on the bait and does all the catching for you including the reeling into shore.

To some extent this is a Citizen Survivor's dream fishing kit, saving a lot of work and effort.

This method gives you an excellent bit of kit to add to your bag – in fact the more of these you can get your hands on the better! Once you set it up you can just leave it to go to work and catch you fish! It's like having a robot helper.

Don't panic if you can't get one of these those, we expect they are rarer then hen's teeth now.

Net Fishing

Net and Hook fishing can be much more productive methods but a net in itself can be a bulky piece of kit and in your bag, would may well take up more space than you wish to give up.!

So the net option is generally not considered unless your base is near a river or your bindle has room for one.

However, if this is an option, a gill net is one of the better choices – this is a very lightweight length of net that is stretched out across a river and forms a barrier for the fish to swim into.

Once set up across a river it can be left to do its own work enabling you to get on with other things. The net itself can be rolled up quite small and is very light but the net length needs to be reasonable (20m plus) to be effective and this means more bulk.

A good piece of kit if we say so ourselves. Assuming you have access to a river where you can get to both sides for setting up and plenty of room in your bindle.

Do bear in mind though, denizens and others may come across your net as it's not the most inconspicuous of items!

Spearing

Look at you with your spear, who do you think you are, King Shaka? All you need now is the loincloth!

To catch a fish by spearing does require some practice as well as a clearish pond or river to actually see the fish in the first place.

It is highly unlikely you will have brought a fishing spear with you so you will need to make one – this is time consuming and requires some skills to perfect.

A fishing spear can also be used as a small animal spear. Fishing spears should be multi-pronged so the spear catches and holds the fish.

A single spear end even though sharpened may not

secure the fish or even penetrate.

However, a fishing spear take a lot of practice to perfect as well as most of the time you may need to wade out into the water which can be both dangerous and mean having to dry your clothes.

Catching fish by the spearing method can also be very time consuming. As a general rule spear fishing is not really recommended as the most productive method for most Citizen Survivors in a survival situation. You're not Johnny Foreigner from the Congo!

Bait
Fortunately, in the wild, there's an abundance of bait available for you to use that will attract fish to the hook – we recommend live bait, as it seems to works better and all you have to do is look around you.

Dig up a few worms or use bugs, even odd fruit or berries will work. It may take a while but something will eventually take your bait.

When you do catch something, consider reusing it as bait again. This way you will attract larger fish.

If you want to be really prepared for we would also suggest scrumping 'lures' and adding them to your pack.

You only really need one or two, but a decent selection of lures will save you time looking for live bait and can give you a better chance of catching larger fish.

If you're really struggling, use your loaf! Lift up a

rock and see what happens? Have you ever lifted up a paving slab in your Nan's garden when you were a little fella? Now you're getting it!

Preparing your catch
There are certain things that will help you when gutting your fish and knowing beforehand how to prepare fish will make the job so much easier.

The most essential tool is a good skinning knife with a gutting hook.

Latex or rubber gloves come in useful to reduce the spread of bacteria that is always present in the fish and animals, so be on the lookout when scrumping. Carry some clean cloths and net bags to carry the fish in that allows airflow to keep the fish cool.

Skinning and gutting an animal or a fish can be done with just about any survival knife – however, being prepared for everything the wild can and will throw at you means having some specialist tools. If you are fortunate enough to scrump a good skinning knife and a good gutting knife it will make your life a whole lot easier.

Before you can eat any fish, you must remove parts that will make you ill first. Gutting and preparing your fish is the number one step. There are several different ways of processing your fish for the grill, some hunters like to remove the head while others like to leave it on – it really is a matter of personal choice.

Before any attempt to cook the fish, you must

remove the innards of the fish. If you don't you'll have guts that can be heard in Timbuktu, if you catch our drift.

Make a slit along the belly and then you can just push your finger into the cavity and simply peel them out. Rinse the inside cavity very well with fresh water. You've still got your clean water right?

Never cook and eat any fish until you have removed all entrails. Cooking fish with any traces of the entrails intact can ruin the meat and you have a very high chance of the fish making you ill.

Ideally, for expediency, it is preferable to cook the whole fish first, and then remove the skin once it is cooked. This will save time and effort as you do not have to scale the fish first. If, however, your plan is to fillet the fish into portions, then it will be necessary to scale the fish first.

The gills and the fins also need to be removed before cooking – the area also needs to be washed out and cleaned.

Learning this skill of preparing a fish properly is a very important Citizen Survivor skill and most definitely one that should be practiced often.

Think back to the water, it's one thing to get it, it's another thing to have it for your supper!

Cooking your fish

Fresh fish needs to be handled carefully and to stop the fish from falling apart when you start to cook it – lay the fish on a flat rock – it only has to be close enough to the fire to maintain heat and it will cook slowly.

Another way to cook your fish is by using several layers of saplings over the fire and support with forked sticks, then simply lay the fish on the saplings to cook. You can also drape or hang your fish over a single sapling that is above the fire. Be warned though, this method tends to make the flesh fall off as it cooks. Having these type of Citizen Survivor skills means you can eat well while in the wild and not become sick.

WOT?
NO FOOD
(IN THE WILD)?

Hunting

Are you sick of the taste of fish yet? Well lucky you, at least you're alive. Now you've got food in your belly let's see what else the wild has on the menu! It's got to be better than the egg and chips they used to serve in the East End! There are many methods of catching your wild food in the wilderness, but knowing how to make snares and traps, is one of the most essential survival skills you will need to learn. While it is more than possible for you to survive for several weeks without any food, it is not generally recommended you go out and try.

Finding game

Lookout for any animal scat, yes, you heard us right, that's your ticket to a hot meal (the owner of the scat, not the scat itself). If you've found animal scat, you've found the area the animal will use on its route to find food. As well as animal scat, the creature may have stopped and eaten something along his daily route – look out for signs of husks and stalks – a sure sign he has passed this way.

You must know the safe procedures to butcher and prepare the food once you have managed to trap, snare or have caught some fish. Any game or fish you catch in the wild must be processed and prepared almost immediately, especially in warm weather, to prevent spoilage. You'll only have a matter of hours before that rabbit you're about to snare is inedible. Let's not get bogged down with that yet though, let's get you that food in the first place!

Snares

Snaring and trapping is designed to kill an animal by either choking, crushing, hanging or entangling the animal until dead, thus making it safe for you to approach the animal. As with all things survival, the most effective traps are usually the simplest – the key to good trapping is knowing and understanding an animal's habits in order to position your traps in the very best places where you have a higher chance of actually catching the animal. Without doubt, good trapping comes down to location, location, location.

A spring snare is ideal because once the animal is snared it is secured out of the reach of any predators (animals at least) prowling the trails. Look for signs of depression in the grass, which indicates an animal trail. To construct a spring snare you will need cordage, a survival knife or small axe, a slender sapling that can be bent, a peg to secure the sapling and a stake that is driven into the ground. The small peg needs a notch or extended elbow so it can be secured to the stake driven into the ground.

Pull the sapling down so there is enough tension for it to spring back up when released. Tie a length of cordage to the sapling and the other end to the small peg and holding the sapling secure the peg to the driven stake so it holds the bent tree in place. Carefully tie another length of string to the peg.

Make a loop with some cordage and make sure you use a slipknot so when an animal's head tries to force its way through the loop it tightens. Take the other end of the string that is attached to the peg and tie it to the loop.

Push some slender sticks into the ground and drape the loop over them so the loop's shape is maintained. Once an animal walks into the snare it will pull the peg loose that is holding the tension on the sapling causing it to spring up with the animal snared.

It will take practice but you'll soon hone your

Citizen Survivor skills to the point where you can set a dozen or so snares in a relatively short period. Avoid making your snares overly complicated as it is time consuming. You need to weigh your efforts against the results when hunting for food, there is no point in expending 1,000 calories only to net 300 calories. Your traps and snares must be such they can be set up in minutes so you can set about searching for other ways to obtain food.

Rabbit soup for dinner anyone? Imagine being able to say that!

A simple snare.
The simple snare is exactly what you would expect it to be, the most basic construction of a trap, using minimum equipment and materials. Knowing how to make a snare to trap animals is relatively easy. In fact a simple snare can be constructed in minutes and is the fastest type of trap to set up; the hard part is working out the best location for the trap to be set.

Looking for animal runs and paths the animal may take can be quite a challenge sometimes. A simple snare is no more than a wire or rope with a sliding noose on one end, and the other end firmly anchored down to something solid. The advantages of using a wire snare is its rigidity and ability to also be flexible enough to close down over the animal. Because of this, the simple snare can be used in several different locations where other traps will fail. Setting several of these almost guarantees successful trapping.

It is recommended that you use wire for a simple snare so it maintains its shape. Wire should be between 20 and 24 gauge with a loose slipknot so the wire tightens easily once the animal tries to force its shoulders through the snare. You have to size your snares for the type of animal you expect to trap otherwise the loop will be either too big or small. A simple snare may not hold the animal long, so check often and to prevent predators from running off with your catch as well.

Keep in mind you are competing with other folk, not to mention wild animals that have been honing their survival skills for years. Place the snares along trails leading to and from water and along small game runs that lead to and from any animal dens. Animals will use more than one trail so always look for the so-called backdoor trail or bolt hole if you discover a den and want to set snares close by.

Deadfall traps

Ominous name, isn't it? Deadfall traps aren't something we really recommend for the Citizen Survivor who is still wet behind the ears. Though it could be useful down the line, it can be complicated and occasionally you can injure yourself setting one up. A trap such as the one depicted can be used for smaller animals and they typically need to be baited because they are difficult to set up along game trails, generally because larger animals along the trail will trip them.

You must bait them to draw the animal to a spot where they would not normally be. Use bait that is not plentiful in the area. There is no point in baiting a trap with acorns when you are in a forest of oak trees because there is no reason for the animal to be attracted to the trap. Use any scraps of last night's supper from your pack. There are numerous components to a deadfall trap making them more complicated to set up than a snare. The more complicated something is the greater chance of a malfunction.

Use deadfalls traps to target specific animals you know are in the area and set them close to where you suspect they might be.

Location and baiting a trap

Even though you now know how to make a snare trap to catch animals for your food, the next important thing is to lure the animal into your snare. Correctly baiting the trap can mean the difference between you getting lunch and the animal walking off with his lunch – provided by you!

Baiting a trap is a whole science in itself, but you don't have the time to worry about that. Let's just say that expert hunters who use snares and traps are always good trackers and know the body language of animals. How animals move about in the wilderness and being able to spot the signs of an active route that the animal uses is a skill on its own and takes quite a while to learn, but there are always signs to be seen, even for a novice hunter.

Firstly, you must look for an area that is highly populated with animals – to do this just look for simple signs on the forest floor and on the trees, for example, are there claw marks? Animals will do all sorts of things as they wander around the forest. Looking out for these signs will give you an idea the routes they take on a regular basis.

The ideal places to set up a snare is along the animals' routes. Checkout the type of berries and leaves that are about and see if there are signs of the animal eating them – if the animal is eating foods that are in the area, then foods not common to the area will attract them into your snare. Plants that are stripped bare are a good indication that there are animals in the area as well as telling you the food they like. Once all their favourite food in the area is eaten they will move on to other foods. Your bait will be as irresistible as an apple pie on the window sill to a recalcitrant schoolboy!

As we previously stated, the whole concept of baiting a trap can become a science in itself – it's certainly something that takes time to learn but essentially, baiting is a combination of your tracking skills and ability to observe your surroundings. Learn the daily life of the forest and the routines of each of the animals, and observe what foods they eat. Robin Hood did it, and look how merry his men were!

Before you begin baiting the trap you should take careful note of what the animals have and have not been eating, as well as to what degree the food reserve has actually gone. With that in mind, the best bait to use in your trap is the one that has been eaten first.

As soon as you find yourself in the wild, reassure yourself that countless creatures survive out there every day. As you develop your basic survival skills as a Citizen Survivor, you will be improving to the point where you know you can obtain food in the wild. Watch out, Jack Jones, there's a new boy in town!

Gutting your catch

Look at you, Timmy Townie is now just about to gut and skin his first animal! You're a regular boy scout and you have come on leaps and bounds! We will use a rabbit for this example, but the technique is similar for all game.

To remove the entrails, start at the tail/anus and cut into the belly and up to the chest cavity. You must take care as you slice into the belly to ensure you do not puncture the entrails. A good skinning knife will come in very handy here – especially a knife with a gut hook. Some good skinning knives will have a gut hook expressly for that purpose, they only penetrate far enough to cut open the layers of skin. Bury all the animal's entrails immediately – that way you will not attract any predators and insects.

Cut the head and feet off and spread the cavity open and prop with a stick then wipe the cavity out. You want the meat to cool as quickly as possible so never leave the entrails in any longer than necessary.

Golly gosh, I bet you've gone green just reading this. It's nothing different to what you've been eating all these years, the only difference is you used to pay someone else to do it for you so stiffen up that upper lip!

Leave the skin on until you are ready to process the meat for cooking.

Skinning your catch

Skinning the animal is easier if you hang it up from its hind legs. Ideally you should use a sharp skinning knife if you have one, otherwise, any hunting knife will have to do. Make a slit in the skin along the backside of the hind legs. Then start to peel the skin off the animal by starting at the hind legs and then working forward, you will pull the skin inside out essentially. The skin can be kept for curing, if you know how, otherwise it must be buried as soon as possible.

To take the limbs off, simply cut through the joints. On small game, the legs will have very little meat on them, however, they should be kept as they can be placed in water and boiled to produce a protein rich broth. Make an incision either side of the backbone and right through the ribs – this will free the breast meat. If you intend to dry some of the meat, place it to one side on the drying rack, otherwise skewer the animal and place over the heat.

Cooking your catch

Survival cooking, or, as some might even call it call it 'primitive cooking' dates back to the beginning of man, because after all, your ancestors in many cases would have used the very methods that will be described here, and they wouldn't have been so grumpy about it!

First, keep in mind that all wild game, fish and insects should be cooked thoroughly before eating, so having a method of cooking is imperative. Food must always be heated to an adequate internal temperature to destroy any parasites and bacteria that can cause illness or worse.

Using your Citizen Survivor skills you must now start a camp fire and then make two spit poles by pushing two forked sticks into the ground on either side of the fire.

Using a slender sapling, simply skewer the animal along its length and lay across the fire supported in the forks. Next you will need to construct a small platform using green saplings – positioned close to the heat, but not over the flames, this is to be used as a curing/drying rack for any of the meat you cannot eat right away. If you have more meat than you can eat lay it across the drying rack, as it is essential to cure any extra meat you have and to preserve it for later. Carry on like this and you'll be opening the first wilderness restaurant!

Other food sources

Insects and other creepy crawlies
Hold on, hear us out, don't look at us like that! We appreciate it's not very Jack Jones but you may find yourself desperate enough to have to do this one day, and insects are a very surprising source of nutrition, provided they are prepared and cooked!

Let's pretend you want to eat them for starters! A nice chubby maggot may look appetising but don't eat him just yet. Avoid just grabbing that nice big fat grasshopper and popping him into your mouth. Insects, like most other species can carry toxins and bacteria that is harmful to humans – in fact if you like the look of slugs, nice big fat juicy slugs, then you've just signed your own death sentence if you eat one raw! Slugs and snails, which are generally considered as insect food by MOS guidelines, can carry the parasite called Rat Lungworm, which, if ingested by a human can induce a form of meningitis which will give you brain damage!

The answer to all insect eating is to always make the effort and cook them first. By steaming or roasting in a pan you will kill off all the bad stuff. Certain insects need to be gutted; just like a fish you need to remove the entrails before cooking as this will spoil the food and give it a very bad taste.

Adding insects to a meal will give you much needed extra protein and can even enhance the flavours. It depends very much on what supplies you have as to how much added flavour you can give to your insects, but some require very little flavouring to be palatable.

The humble ant, of which there are literally billions under our feet is a good example of an insect that is both readily available, easy to catch and cook, and tastes quite nice. You can catch ants by leaving a stick over an ant hill or along an ant run and within minutes you will have them crawling all over it. Simply shake into a covered pan and repeat until you have a pan full. Roast over a fire until crisp. Ants give off a mild secretion when they feel threatened which is pleasantly sour, rather like vinegar. Add a bit of sugar if you have it, and you've got yourself sweet and sour ants.....

Crickets and Grasshoppers are another insect easily

caught – place a jar on its side and bait it with a piece of apple or similar, a tiny drop of beer also works. By morning it will be full of them – dry them out in the sun for a day and then they will be ready for your pan to be freshly fried.

Earthworms are another species in abundance if you can entice them out of the ground. They appear when it rains and they come up for air before they drown! You can simulate this by digging a hole and filling with water and soaking the surrounding ground – they will soon show themselves.

Collect them as they are very nutritious and easily cooked in a hot pan – they will be a bit bitter though. Before cooking, you need to purge them by soaking in water for a couple of hours and then hold with one hand and squeeze the dirt out with the other.

Maggots are the superfood of the insect world. Maggots are extremely fatty and a rich source of essential amino acids, making them nutritionally far more valuable than lean meat. You could even grow your own by leaving out some meat to go rancid. Your maggot will have different flavours depending on what it has been feeding on and is an acquired taste. But worth it!

Go on, don't be a prude, give it a go! It's a brave new world!

Nuts, berries, fruit, mushrooms and all that malarkey

We're not going to go into all this, just use your loaf and a bit of common sense. As we mentioned earlier, if in doubt, LEAVE WELL ALONE! It is better to avoid mushrooms completely unless you know what you're doing as some of them can be poisonous. Whether berries are worth the calories burnt collecting is a choice for you to make. However, taking a few pears or apples from fruit trees along the way is an obvious no brainer.

If possible, scrump books on foraging for these food items.

Wrapping food
You're doing well at this we hope, all you need now is your pith helmet and blunderbuss and you're like a little Victorian explorer!

To add flavour you can wrap your food with dandelion leaves and buds and the unopened buds from burdock. Add the roots of an arrowroot plant and then steam to tenderness along with your game or fish. Wrapping foods in burdock leaves or bulrushes also helps contain the heat and will tenderize the fish or game you are cooking and the leaves can be eaten along with the game or fish. Burdock leaves make excellent wraps for your food and the roots were considered a delicacy in many cultures.

Do not wash or clean the roots until ready to prepare for eating.
You cannot use poisonous plant leaves for cooking wraps and obviously, you cannot eat them.

One thing that is greatly overlooked by scrumpers are books, books are priceless. Not your top shelf nonsense that the missus used to read while you were having a few pints, but proper education books. If you ever find one, try to get a botany guide on edible plants. It's not likely many people have been scrumping in libraries so it's worth a shot. Take time to read this book when you can (after you've finished this one of course).

Cooking with fire

We have already covered fire (you haven't forgotten already have you?), but here is a very quick glance at a couple of effective cooking methods.

Fire Pits

A fire pit is the most effective way to cook because the fire is enclosed and the heat is concentrated upward. You can lay green saplings over the top of the pit to use as cooking racks and the high moisture content in the saplings can help cook the foods; this is similar to plank cooking.

The method involves digging a small depression in the ground using whatever equipment you may have – if you have none, then this can still be done with your bare hands or a good stick. Next, lay flat rocks in the hole and build your fire on top. Let the fire burn down to coals and then scrap away the coals and lay your food that has been wrapped in leaves on top of the hot rocks. Layer grasses on top of the wrapped food and allow the heat to create steam from the grasses and leaves and you can essentially poach your food.

If you have the tools, you can split cedar or oak

saplings and lay the pieces cut side up over the pit to use the planks as a cooking surface. This will also infuse the moisture and flavour in the wood into the food.

Dakota Fire Hole

To make your fire pit more efficient you can build what is called a Dakota fire hole, this requires no equipment at all, just your hands and a good digging stick broken from a tree. It relies on an air chamber, which provides oxygen to the fire pit making it extremely efficient and reduces the amount of fuel needed.

Once the pit is constructed, you can use a spit method for cooking or lay flat rocks slightly over the edge to heat and use as a cooking surface or use green saplings or planks as a cooking surface.

Beggars can't be choosers

You may find your equipment merely consists of a mess tin, a wooden bowl or possibly nothing more than a piece of plastic or canvas. You can use anyone of these to boil water in to cook your food.

Cooking with hot rocks

Build a fire and choose your rocks carefully because rocks with high moisture content will fragment under heat and they can splinter and fly out of the fire. Use granite or quartz and again make sure the rocks will fit into the container. If all you have is canvas or plastic sheets dig a shallow depression and line with the canvas or plastic, fill with water and place the hot rocks in the water.

Heat the rocks for at least an hour in the fire and then carefully place the hot rocks in the container of water along with whatever food you have. Hopefully, you've scrumped your fair share of tools and kit by now. This will help make your survival so much easier and help with moving the hot rocks, as well as digging and finding fire making materials.

Tools such as a machete or camp axe are perfect to slide the rocks on to and be moved. Start with several rocks to first to get an idea of how many you will need to heat the water enough to cook your foods. Have rocks as backup that can replace the ones you remove.

Essentially you can (in theory) survive without any equipment it just takes a bit longer and is much harder work.

Excerpt from the MOS sponsored radio show 'The Adventures of Jack Jones'.

Narrator:
Ladies and gentleman, the adventures of Jack Jones (title music; audience applause). Jack comes across a nasty bunch of bullies. Four of them surround him with their knives.

Jack:
Whatcha' guv (audience laughter).

Bully 1:
'Ere, none of that. Hand over the bag and we'll let you live (audience booing).

Jack:
Hang about, hang about. 'Ere what are you wearing, you look like you're off to the ball? (Audience laughter)

Bully 2:
Come on now, or we'll stick you

Jack:

I've got nothing you want, why do you think I'm on the road, I'm not doing it for my health am I? (Audience laughter)

Bully 3:
Give it to 'im boss.

Jack:
Hold on a bloomin' minute lads. Tell me what you want?

Bully 1:
Grub, cigarettes and alcohol.

Jack:
Holing up for the winter then are you? (Audience laughter) You don't want to waste your time on me, and I don't have any of what you're after and I take it you're the sort of chaps who'd sell their rods for a plate of cod and chips. Back that way, there's a thatched cottage at the cross-roads. Elderly couple there, said 'ello to me. They've got a stockpile of whiskey.

Bully 2:
What shall we do, guv?

Bully 1:
Bloody 'ellfire, on your way then. You look flat broke anyway.

Narrator:
The four bully boys wander off and leave Jack to it (audience applause).

Jack:
Bloomin' idiots. Good job I always carry me Ministry of Survivors handbook (audience applause), that'll tell you all you need to know. Misinformation and lies is the oldest trick in the book, there's nothing to be gained from sharing information or telling the truth. Remember keep mum! (Audience applause)

Narrator:
Lucky Jack continues on his way.

Jack:
Whatcha' (audience applause).

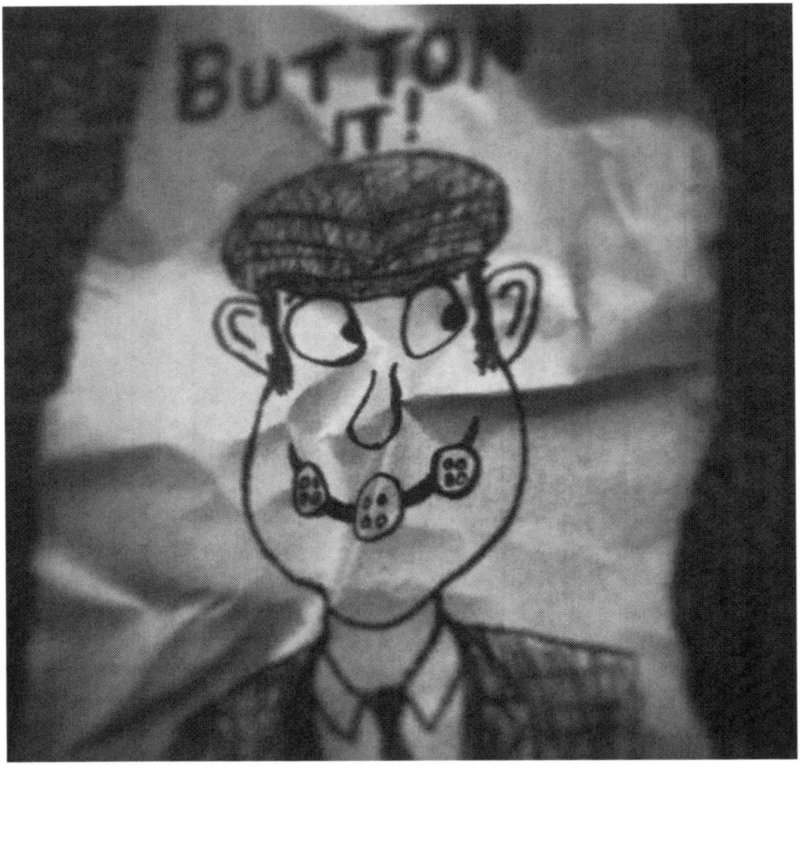
BUTTON
IT!

HYGIENE SANITATION AND FIRST-AID

"Wash yourselves; make yourselves clean; remove the evil of your deeds from before my eyes; cease to do evil."
– Isaiah 1:16; Church of the Remnant

Keep clean, keep sane
Yes, yes, it may not be Sunday bath time but you still need to keep clean. A nice, hot bath may seem like a distant memory now but it's not impossible to recreate. Cleanliness is next to godliness so they say, and it is more important than you think to stop infection and disease. Particularly women with all their peculiar anatomical curiosities.

The subjects of personal hygiene, waste management and rubbish disposal are high up on the survival list, especially in the wild as it can be the very thing that can brings everything else to a grinding halt, and your survival skills must prepared to keep your personal hygiene to a level where you are at the minimum risk of infection, disease and illness.

It becomes even more essential when considering your waste management and what to do with it. Come now, let's not be prudish, we're beyond that! Yes, yes, we know it's a bit of a gross subject. But you must learn about sanitation now. Excuse the pun, you must learn the ins and outs…!

The three main areas to be concerned with are:

- Personal hygiene – cleanliness and personal sanitation
- General waste & rubbish disposal
- Human waste & waste management

Personal hygiene
Personal hygiene can actually mean both inside and outside the body. Inside will include drinking safe, sterile water that's free from parasites and viruses and water that will not make you sick.

Outside the body, e.g. your skin, requires special attention as it is very easy to get an infected cut that has the possibility to turn septic. If this cannot be treated, the wound can easily escalate into a very serious condition requiring medical treatment and some serious drugs. As they won't be available to you, you can guess how that one ends! If you are in an abandoned home with a bath tub, then you can have a bath. You already know how to boil water, so work out the rest! Only ever give in to this decadent, time and water consuming luxury if water is plentiful and not a concern to you.

Locating a water source is important for both drinking water and water to wash with. If you have to conserve your water, you still need to keep clean –

certainly in the groin, armpit area and especially your hands. Hopefully you have scrumped a decent first aid kit. But at the very least you should try to ensure that you have antiseptics and an ointments kit to both clean any wounds, bites or stings and then be able to apply antibiotic cream to the wound. Again, these things are easier to scrump then you'd think, as bully denizens to not tend to think beyond the day today.

General waste & rubbish disposal
You must be sensible with everything you throw away – in your situation this could be anything from chewing gum to an animal carcass. It is absolutely necessary to dispose of it with care and in the correct manner.

Building up a pile of rubbish all around your camp is never a good idea. It could cause a potential risk to your health, and increase the risk of wild animals sniffing around your camp at night and using you as their food store. It will also alert any undesirables to your location. You really must try and contain all general waste in one place, preferably in a plastic bag AND AWAY FROM YOUR CAMP and ensure your rubbish disposal methods leave no trace.

Burn what you can on your fire that evening, and as for the rest, why not dig a hole a fair walk from your site?

Human waste
In the area of human waste, you have several choices – the choices depend on how comfortable you are with

the wilderness or how comfortable you want to be. In your situation, your human waste management is quite easy – you find a private part of the woods, away from your camp, dig a hole and fill it in after – finished. It's important you fill it in, nothing gives away a Citizen Survivor like a fresh, warm poo. Don't forget, you will still need to wipe. We appreciate it is not ideal or particularly aesthetic but you may have designated old clothing for this job.

Injury, disease and infection are very real threats in the wild – So eliminating the chances of getting any of them are very important to your survival. Failure in any area of personal hygiene and your decisions as to your methods of waste management are crucial areas and will result in very unpleasant viruses and illness and in a prolonged untreated situation, and will, most definitely, put you at severe risk of infection.

Insect bites

Bugs and all the other nasties can cause you serious infection. At the very least, they can drive you doolally as they bite away all day and all night; do not underestimate the effect this will have on your mental state – it is important to prepare for this. It is always worth trying to scrump for an insect repellent spray. This is easier than you think as most scrumpers seem to overlook it. Particularly one that contains deet, designed to repel ticks, mosquitoes, chiggers and biting flies, and is made for extreme environments. Spray of any sort can also be used for self-defence - sprays containing Deet will produce burning to the eyes and give a nasty surprise to any rogues!

If you get stung by a bee use a knife blade or fingernail to scrape the stinger out, but never squeeze because this will release more venom into your system.

If stung or bitten mix mud and wood ash together and dab on the area, or use cold compresses if available and if nothing else is available cover with a piece of cloth dipped in water. You may also find relief by crushing dandelion leaves or the flower stem and rubbing the sap on the area to soothe the sting or bite.

However, in the first instance, you should try to ensure you can administer immediate relief from a sting or bite without resorting to foraging around. Try to scrump for a good ammonia based after bite remedy. Again, not the first choice of pickings for bully denizens!

A tick bite should be treated immediately as they are dangerous – once bitten it is important to monitor the area for sign of further infection. Ticks transmit Lyme disease and any signs of redness or inflammation around the infected area must be treated by a doctor immediately, so we're sure you can understand what a big problem this could be for you. Ticks should always be removed as soon as possible and pulled out fully intact with the body and head still attached. Pulling only the tick body out will leave the head attached, which can cause infections. Do not squeeze the tick – this will cause it to vomit straight into your blood system, and once removed wash the area and your hands well.

Spider bites must be cleaned immediately to prevent bacteria from getting into the wound.

Although next to impossible in Blighty, it's worth remembering a scorpion or spider bite can cause anaphylactic shock in some cases though it is rare. Death is quite rare in most cases involving spiders and scorpions but it is possible if the victim has underlying medical conditions.

First aid
Let's not get too bogged down with first aid; you're a Citizen Survivor, it's not like you can pop into St. Bartholomew's for a check-up! However, let's concentrate on keeping you alive and avoiding little injuries turning into big problems! Also, we're not going to talk about the recovery position, how to treat burns and all that nonsense. There are other books for all that. Besides, why would you want to help a stranger anyway? So they can recover and steal your bindle? No thank you!

Assessing your personal medical requirements and also the requirements of your family is a very big responsibility. There is nothing more soul destroying for a Citizen Survivor then seeing a loved one pass on because of what was initially a trivial and minor injury.

If you are in good health and do not need to take any tablets or have injections or need medication on a regular basis then you are one of the lucky ones. Your chances of survival have just increased a thousand percent! If not, well, bless you for giving it a go! If there were medals for tenacity, you'd get one! Typically, diabetes is one of them – as a Citizen Survivor you would have to scrump a hell of a lot of medication, and even then you're only delaying the inevitable, because no one's making any more of the stuff.

Injuries and immediate medical procedures are very necessary survival skills for Citizen Survivors. It is very easy to learn and master the basics of first aid and how to administer medial help to yourself and others.

It shouldn't be too difficult to put together a good first aid medical kit that will cater for most emergency situations.

First aid kits
Even a half decent first aid kit is a blessing. Even cutting your thumb without a plaster can turn a good day sour. However, the best first aid kits cannot just be thrown together, it must be thought out to ensure

emergency first aid equipment is the most appropriate for your situation. There is no such thing as a standard first aid kit.

There are many types of first aid kits out there for scrumping that come close to what you may need, but it is pretty certain you will need to add to and improve this in readiness for your particular situation.

An example would be if you foresee hiking out into the forest, then you must carry insect bite creams and anti-histamine creams, as well as protection for stings and bites. Maybe consider good tweezers for splinters and even a good magnifying glass to help see them.

Your location plays a big part in putting together your first aid kit – and what about the weather? Your kit needs to be seasonal as well, so this will mean changing the contents to ensure you have the correct items for first aid. This could mean scrumping sun block lotions and creams, lip balm and aftersun creams too.

Although rarer than hen's teeth, if you come across a product called 'quick clot', scrump it! For large blood flow this stuff will coagulate the blood very quickly. Scrump medical supplies whenever you can, they shouldn't take up too much room in your bindle. In particular, we recommend you keep a look out for the following items in addition to the normal inventory.
- Several extra pairs of latex gloves – in medium & large sizes.
- Antiseptic hand wipes and/or hand wash gel – for cleaning hands before & after an incident.

- Surgical masks – to reduce the transfer of air born contaminates.
- Pack of adhesive sutures – to close serious wounds.
- Scalpel – avoid using your survival knife – a sterile scalpel for removing tissue, minor surgery.
- Super glue – if you need to close a wound fast.
- Duct tape – an essential item for everything.

This list and more could go on and on but being prepared with some emergency first equipment is better than none. If possible, try to add some antibiotics to your bindle. If you can't scrump antibiotics, try fish antibiotics (yes, you heard us right, Citizen Survivor!). They are the same product and contain the same ingredients.

Remember Citizen Survivor, don't panic! Hopefully you'll never need any of the above, but they are always useful to have if you can. Remember, we've all got a date in the diary, so if you are beyond first aid, give yourself a pat on the back for getting so far in the first place!

Excerpt from the MOS sponsored radio show 'The Adventures of Jack Jones'.

Narrator:
Ladies and gentleman, the adventures of Jack Jones (title music; audience applause). Jack has been avoiding the advances of a good time girl, Jill, as she rolls in the hay with him (audience laughter).

Jack:
Whatcha' guv (audience laughter).

Jill:
Oh come on Jack, I'm gasping for a bit of how's your father.

Jack:
There's only one roll in the hay I want.

Jill:
Let's blinkin' get on with it then!

Jack:

Not that, a sausage roll! (Audience laughter)

Jill:
But I'm a woman Jack, with needs, and I need a big strong man like you to look after me.

Jack:
You seem like a lovely girl, perish the thought, but who knows what countless diseases you're carrying. I'll be itching all the way to John o' Groats (audience laughter). And what about the other?

Jill:
I've been trying to get a bit of the other for the last ten minutes (audience laughter).

Jack:
No you bloomin' idiot, imagine if you got pregnant, that's a death sentence for you and the dustbin lid!

Jill:
Well you could always –

(There is an interruption in the broadcast. A man's voice can be heard shouting)

Man:
Do not believe the lies and propaganda of the Ministry! The Church of the Remnant are here to help, they are your salvation, we welcome everyone, we can

Excerpt from the MOS sponsored radio show 'The Adventures of Jack Jones'.

Narrator:
Ladies and gentleman, the adventures of Jack Jones (title music; audience applause). Jack has been avoiding the advances of a good time girl, Jill, as she rolls in the hay with him (audience laughter).

Jack:
Whatcha' guv (audience laughter).

Jill:
Oh come on Jack, I'm gasping for a bit of how's your father.

Jack:
There's only one roll in the hay I want.

Jill:
Let's blinkin' get on with it then!

Jack:

Not that, a sausage roll! (Audience laughter)

Jill:
But I'm a woman Jack, with needs, and I need a big strong man like you to look after me.

Jack:
You seem like a lovely girl, perish the thought, but who knows what countless diseases you're carrying. I'll be itching all the way to John o' Groats (audience laughter). And what about the other?

Jill:
I've been trying to get a bit of the other for the last ten minutes (audience laughter).

Jack:
No you bloomin' idiot, imagine if you got pregnant, that's a death sentence for you and the dustbin lid!

Jill:
Well you could always –

(There is an interruption in the broadcast. A man's voice can be heard shouting)

Man:
Do not believe the lies and propaganda of the Ministry! The Church of the Remnant are here to help, they are your salvation, we welcome everyone, we can

feed and shelter you, and there are still communities in –

(There is a sustained beeping noise for twelve seconds, and then classical music)

WOT?
NO WEAPONS &
 DEFENCE?

WEAPONS AND DEFENCE

"He shall judge between the nations, and shall decide disputes for many peoples; and they shall beat their swords into ploughshares, and their spears into pruning hooks; nation shall not lift up sword against nation, neither shall they learn war anymore."
– Isaiah 2:4; Church of the Remnant

An introduction to weapons and defence
[Omitted by order of the MOS]

How to communicate with servicemen
[Removed from this edition of the handbook as no longer relevant.]

Becoming a serviceman
[Removed from this edition of the handbook as no longer relevant.]

What is expected of you as a serviceman?
[Removed from this edition of the handbook as no longer relevant.]

Bully denizens
[Omitted by order of the MOS]

Mob rule
[Omitted by order of the MOS]

Community Militia Squadrons (CMS)
[Removed from this edition of the handbook as no longer relevant.]

Self-defence
[Omitted by order of the MOS]

Self-defence for women
[Omitted by order of the MOS]

Defending your home
[Omitted by order of the MOS]

When to fight
[Omitted by order of the MOS]

Long ranged weapons
[Omitted by order of the MOS]

Guns and firearms
[Removed from this edition of the handbook as no longer relevant.]

Crafting a bow
[Omitted by order of the MOS]

Crafting arrows
[Omitted by order of the MOS]

Using a bow
[Omitted by order of the MOS]

Hunting catapults

Remember playing with your own catapults in the woods? Wasn't it grand? Well, it was for the best you did, because the simple catapult will become one of your best friends. For some people, hunting with a catapult has been a lifelong process. But for quite a few people, actually knowing how to accurately shoot a catapult is not quite as easy as it seems!

One of the oldest weapons used for hunting has got to be the catapult and a very good bit of kit to have in your bindle. Hunting catapults can be made from very basic materials and with practice can be very effective. Firstly, let's look at the pros and cons of adding a hunting catapult to your bindle – along with your survival knife and a multi tool knife, a hunting catapult is basic, its principle design and operation, relying more on your own skill than the actual catapult itself.

Do not overlook the importance of a good hunting catapult. Carrying a catapult with you is not only good for hunting, it is good for personal defence, and will make the more cowardly bully denizens think twice before trying to give you a bloody nose.

Dangers and disadvantages of catapults
- Practice required to build up accuracy.
- Ammunition can be bulky and weighty [200x .3in ball bearings would weigh about 1.5lb].
- A supply of replacement catapult bands is required.

It is very important to think of a catapult just like any other weapon – any catapult will very easily injure, maim and even kill a human; they are most definitely not toys, especially when you consider that they are specifically designed to hurl a projectile at some very impressive speeds with an inertia that will do some serious damage. Remember, even presenting your catapult when engaging with other folks will be seen as a sign of hostility and will quickly turn the conversation sour. You really do not want to find yourself on the receiving end of a stone or steel ball bearing travelling a hundreds of feet per second! So think twice before firing it at anyone. Is it not simpler just to run, hide and avoid these folks in the first place?

If you have women or children in your group, do not let them use your catapult, they won't have the ability, understanding or restraint of knowing how and when to use that. Save all that for the chaps!

Advantages of catapults
- Accurate and deadly
- Very quiet operation
- Easy to load and reload
- Fast reload [with practice]
- Simple operation
- Compact
- Light weight
- Main working parts are easily repaired
- Unlimited supply of ammunition (stones)

Your catapult will offer you a simple and effective way to go out into the woods and be able to learn how to stalk your prey, without carrying around lots of cumbersome equipment, weapons and ammo – essentially it is an extremely lightweight, compact, very easy to use, hunting tool Add to that, a catapult can be very accurate and great fun to use. All Citizen Survivors want a clean, fast kill, you're not some vile townie – that's why it is so necessary to actually practice and get yourself proficient with your weapon well before you actually go out into the wild looking for game to hunt.

Fortunately for you, you will find that some animals and birds, especially rabbits and pheasants will tend to hold still long enough for you to take a good aim and some will even allow a second shot if needed. But again, we cannot overstate the need and importance of practice. It is essential that you are more than able to reproduce the firing action and technique you use when plinking at a target – regular practice will ensure you build up 'muscle memory' and use exactly the same action when your heart's pumping and you're all crouched up on the ground trying to aim at your prey for real.

Making a catapult
So simple is it in its design and function that it very rarely goes wrong and a missed shot is mostly the shooter's fault. Although a catapult can be made from various materials, if you're in woodland then you can pick and choose your perfect design. You will always need to choose a branch to make to frame from live wood, still attached to the tree. Dead wood is not as good, especially very old wood – do not use, it will snap and cause injury to you.

Possibly the most difficult part of the catapult is acquiring the actual power bands that propel the stone to take down your prey. Making the rest is quite easy. In its very basic form you only really need two parts for a successful catapult that will give a kill shot. The frame and the power band – the power band can double up as the pouch to hold your stone if really needed. However, a pouch will give extra comfort and a better way to hold your stone. You can make a very crude catapult without any tools, it will look rather Robinson Crusoe, but will work with practice.

Make sure you cut a piece of tree that is man enough in diameter to withstand the tension on its limbs, so the point where the two limbs separate out from the branch must be a solid with the two limbs coming out as symmetrically as possible, this gives maximum strength to the catapult.

Size the frame to fit your hand where maximum grip and stability will make it easy to control without shaking when you pull the band back.

In its simplest form, the rubber power bands can be tied around the limbs to form a loop over each limb or to the inside of each limb. The choice is yours, but whatever you choose you will soon be getting an accurate shot with practice.

Carrying spare power bands is essential, but if you do not have any in the first place you'll need to improvise. Ideally tubular rubber power bands are by far the best choice. They will give a more reliable shot each time. Knicker elastic will not work, nor will a load of elastic bands, so don't try it, they will snap and probably twang you in the eye.

Your best next bet is to use something like a bicycle inner tube (assuming you are lucky enough to scrump one) and cut it into a strip – whether you use one thick strip or several thin ones is up to you, but by experimenting you will find the best draw weight for yourself. If you didn't think to scrump one before they all but disappeared, keep that general thought in mind when choosing an alternative; what you want is something strong but flexible which won't break in normal use. By using one thick strip you can use the rubber as the pouch holder all in one, thus eliminating a weak point in the rubber by additional cuts, but if you do want to make a pouch to hold a stone, then simple cut a piece of material from your clothes – maybe cut off the back pocket of your jeans, trim to shape, pierce two holes in it and thread the band through with a knot to form your new pouch.

Then it's a simple matter of just practice, practice, practice and then some more practice. From here on, you will need to hone your stalking skills – you must get close enough to the animal to fire an effective, accurate shot before he sees you and runs. Stalking is a whole new ball game!

Practice makes perfect

You will, most definitely, find yourself experimenting with different types of ammo sizes and even shapes – as well as changing the power band strength to see what really works best for you. To really improve in your catapult accuracy you must practice, and you can use anything. If you use ball bearings for ammo, then we would suggest weaning yourself off these and learning to shoot stones instead. It's only a matter of time before you run out.

An average quality hunting catapult will very easily take down many of the smaller animals like rabbits, pigeons, squirrels and pheasants – AT CLOSE RANGE. Essentially, that is where the actual skill comes in, you really do need to learn how to silently stalk your prey and then ensure you can get nice and close to make a clean shot.

There is not much to say on this rather than just get practising, and find your own style that works for you.

Technique
Whether you're left or right handed makes no difference when it comes to shooting and firing a hunting catapult properly – what does make a difference is finding a firing position, stance and technique that suits you personally. As a general rule, most people will pull the pouch straight back to around the chin area, below the 'aiming' eye, with a straight arm holding the catapult body.

Remember to think about 'tweaking' your catapult to suit you – well, the power bands need to be adjusted to give you just the right amount of 'stretch' to ensure you are not struggling to pull back, especially over the last few inches. You must be able to comfortably pull back to achieve maximum power without having to struggle – if you find you cannot hold the pouch 'fully cocked' without wobbling then you must extend the band length to suit your body size, strength and style.

It is far better to give away a bit of power than constantly struggle with the band force and subsequently miss your target.

As you get more confident and muscle memory kicks in, you will find it becomes easier to maintain a constant aim with less effort.

Ammunition
This is an area where some people prefer to use large ammo and others smaller – there's no definitive answer to ammo size or type. It makes sense to practice with all types and sizes of stones.

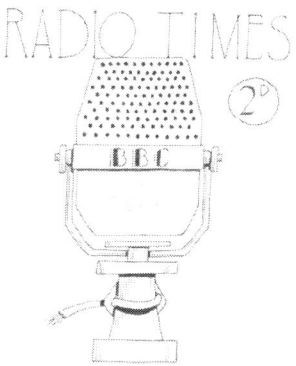

Excerpt from the MOS sponsored radio show 'The Adventures of Jack Jones'.

```
             Narrator:
 Ladies and gentleman, the adventures of
     Jack Jones (title music; audience
   applause). Jack comes across a large
 group of people, one of them is carrying
         a child bound in rope.

              Jack:
   Whatcha' guv (audience laughter).

              Man:
 Hello squire, lovely day for scrumping.

              Jack:
 It is that. Jack Jones, pleased to make
 your acquaintance. What's going on with
 the dustbin lid all roped up, if you're
   playing cowboys and Indians I think the
       cowboys won! (Audience laughter)

              Man:
 We found him by the side of the road,
 crying for his mother he was, the poor
```

blighter.

Jack:
'Ere what's your name, sonny?

Boy:
Ivor, sir.

Jack:
Ivor mind to give you a clip round the ear (audience laughter). How did you get separated from your family?

Ivor:
I was just playing, my family's camp is only an hour or so away.

Jack:
Well, did you have any signals, any communications, any emergency plans?

Ivor:
Afraid not, sir.

Jack:
Blimey, you've got less chance finding your family then I've got winning the bingo (audience laughter).

Ivor:
I want to look for them, they are my family! Please, let me go!

Jack:
You're better off with these chaps now, lad.

IVOR:
They just took me, it's not right, I've been kidnapped. They bound me in rope when I tried to run.

JACK:
Well that's your luck now, lad. Here have a read of this handbook from the Ministry of Survivors (audience applause), that'll tell you all you need to know. Make sure you don't get lost again.

IVOR:
Can't I go with you? Won't you help me look for my family?

JACK:
'Ere I'm Jack Jones, I travel alone, don't you know. You can keep the book for your troubles though. I'll have a look for your folks when I've finished looking for my needle I lost in a haystack (audience laughter). These folk are your family now, and best to be a good boy now or they'll do you in.

IVOR:
What a prize idiot I've been. I'd be brown bread without you!

JACK:
If you were brown bread I'd butter you myself (audience laughter). Speaking of which, I better scarper, before I find any strays myself.

Man:
Thank you, Jack Jones.

Jack:
Whatcha'! (Audience applause).

SIGNALLING AND COMMUNICATION

"By your words you will be acquitted, and by your words you will be condemned."."
– Matthew 12:37; Church of the Remnant

Gassing with the neighbours

As we've said countless times, why on earth do you want to signal and communicate with strangers? Nothing good will come of it. However, we understand every Citizen Survivor has their own set of individual circumstances and you may be travelling in a group who you are split up from. Therefore, we've had decided to keep this information from the first edition in, though it has been heavily edited, but use it at your peril. If you go looking for snakes you might just find them!

Citizen Survivors do often form packs (more on that to come), but the MOS do advise extreme caution on this for reasons we will discuss later.

Remember Citizen Survivor – Those seemingly nice folks may not be so dumb. Keep mum!

Communication

Communication between fellow citizens can be useful we concede, but only in very exceptional circumstances. We all know the importance of keeping a low profile and operating below the radar.

The same applies even more during times of violence, chaos and panic when you have to get out quick and survive as best you can, away from the crowds of terrified, desperate townies and raging bully denizens hell bent on getting your bindle at any cost. As you move further away from urban environments, there will come a time when things start to quieten down. Also, take comfort that time is a healer, these folks who get by on yesterday's goods have no tomorrow. We will reach a point of equilibrium where only the strongest and most prepared Citizen Survivors are surviving. Yes, there will still be those who've gone doolally, but one glorious day, folk like you will be majority!

If you are a family who have bugged out together, then having a means of communication and signalling between yourselves is essential to your continued survival. If you have a survival plan with other Citizen Survivors then you must ensure you have the will and means to put that plan into operation. There are many methods of communicating between two people – some covert and some not, but either way communication must be set up at some point.

Basic signalling is an essential skill to learn – as with all aspects of survival, the simpler the better. Reduce the risk of equipment failure by keeping the equipment you use as simple as possible. Signalling and communication between yourselves and others is something you must learn quickly before any disaster and ensuring you are prepared with the basic equipment must be part of your bindle.

Remember, if you get split up from your loved ones, it'll be a miracle if you ever see them again or get to them before someone else does with intentions not as honourable as yours!

Rescue and reunion
Ideally, you want to lay low; out of sight, out of mind. No harm, no foul as the old saying goes. Going unnoticed is one of the key skills in your situation, especially if the situation has required you to scarper quickly, away from looting and unrest and potentially highly dangerous people who need food and water at all costs. For a Citizen Survivor your signalling and communication skills will generally (we hope) be restricted to your family and close, trusted friends (more on trust later).

In a situation where you actually WANT to be found or rescued, your signalling and communication skills need to be much higher up on your list of Citizen Survivor priorities. Pre-arranged signalling between family members is needed to ensure your safety and communication. As usual, these must be prepared way in advance – practiced and understood between all parties, and any equipment needed must be stored away in your bindles.

Methods of signalling include; hand signals; whistles

and flags. Signalling over a distance includes mirrors and fire. You can also break down signalling methods into manageable pieces, for example, some signalling requires you physically do something, like make a hand gesture – this is generally known as ACTIVE SIGNALLING. Other methods, like forming an SOS sign on a beach or with rocks, is considered to be STATIC SIGNALLING (there is no point doing this by the way).

Remember, we are dealing with a Citizen Survivor approach to signalling here – requiring a more covert approach over the usual 'look everyone, I'm over here, come and get me' scenario. Being found by strangers is probably going to be much worse than not being found at all.

Hand signals
Hand signals are by far the most effective methods of signalling as they are noiseless and relatively simple. Their downside is that both parties have to be within eyesight of each other and know what each signal means. But you really only need to know a few hand signals to get by. They can be the same as the textbooks or even make your own up – but get something done so you can communicate silently with your family if you are in danger.

Do not bother yourself with old military hand signals; as long as you and your loved ones understand what you are communicating that is all that matters. For instance, two hands up straight could mean 'hide', or a right fist out straight may mean 'come here', but work it out among yourselves.

Whistles

A whistle is a good item to carry in any situation as it is very light and compact and has next to no moving parts that can go wrong. The loud shrill is also more than enough to get attention if needed. Though think about whose attention you may be getting. You can also control the volume of a whistle quite easily with a little practice making this a good way of communicating.

One of the good things about a whistle is they are relatively easy to scrump.

Flags

Perhaps a bit advanced for the journeyman Citizen Survivor, but worth knowing. Flags are another excellent signalling method. They don't need to be a huge flag either – just a small bit of cloth will do. At their basic level, red would equal danger. You can also use material of different shapes to indicate different messages. e.g.: a square white could mean 'left' and a triangle white equal 'right'.

They can be used to secretly guide you and your loved ones back to your base – or for complete signalling, there's always the internationally recognised signalling method of Semaphore. Information on this should be scrumped from libraries.

Mirrors

Mirror signalling is good for short and long distance

communication and requires relatively little sunlight to produce good results. Again the beauty of a mirror for signalling, is size and weight, easily fitting in your bindle or even in your pocket. At worst, any old reflective surface will do (the end of a can, some broken glass) – the inside of your old tobacco tin is also a very good makeshift signalling mirror.

Again you do not need to know the whole signalling codes, but a few will definitely help you to communicate better.

Fire
Slow down, Sitting Bull! Who do you think you are? Fires are a lot less covert than the other methods mentioned here so far, but need to be included for pure positioning and location reasons.

A fire can be a bad idea if you are trying to stay concealed and it requires a lot of skill to hide the smoke it gives off. Smoke can be seen for miles and will lead anyone straight to your camp. Not a great idea if you want to stay unnoticed (which we hope and expect you do!). However, there may be a situation where you are desperate to be reunited, at whatever cost. So making smoke from a fire could be your best shot.

Flares
Flares only really serve one purpose – to indicate a position of an emergency or pick up point; in an old rescue situation they were okay, but not really useful for Citizen Survivors. Again, let's wean ourselves off yesterday's technology.

Daubings

You will likely come across many infantile and bizarre daubings painted onto buildings and signs. Ignore these, these are the mad ramblings of bully denizens and whatever nonsense these signs meant when created, the message is probably already out of date. The only sign you should keep an eye out for can be best described as a septagram. This is generally used to warn people of the Church of the Remnant, so stay well clear and scarper!

Radio

While technically not communication, on your front at least, we have decided to maintain some small parts from the first handbook in relation to radio channels that may still be broadcasting.

British Public Alert System (BPAS)

[Removed from this edition of the handbook as no longer relevant.]

Whitehall Radio

[Removed from this edition of the handbook as no longer relevant.]

Witford Radio – 1570khz MW

Bizarrely, there are still two radio stations that operate at the time of publication. One of these is Witford radio. Days and weeks can pass with radio silence, but Witford Radio does still play. Witford Radio was originally created by the philanthropic Witford sisters as a morale booster. It is not known how or even if the radio station is still monitored, as the station plays the same playlist on repeat without interference. Although the situation may have changed by the time you read this, we have included this peculiarity for posterity. We do not recommend listening to this station, as nothing will give away your position faster than The Laughing Policeman playing from just one house in an abandoned village. It's easy to forget just how silent the countryside is when you've been a cooped-up townie all your life!

British union of survivors radio (BUS RADIO) – 700khz MW

We do not recommend listening to this station under any circumstances, in fact, we strongly advise against it, it'll drive you to despair. It only appears to broadcast for a few minutes a day and again at night. As mentioned before, the situation has likely changed by the time you read this. BUS radio is essentially the old and eccentric Earl Wathmere (Lord Wind-bag) of the British Union of Survivors waffling about nothing. Ignore his mad, vitriolic, inane, drunken ramblings - don't let him fill your head with gobbledygook!

Here is an example of his nonsense:

```
"Wathmere calling, Wathmere calling.
What foul heresy. What blatant disregard.
With honed guts and tensed sinews that I
should consider this the form of it all,
carved from hideous oak and placed in the
hands of undeserving Shylocks. With such
foul force that their odious nature
should fester in the clothes and upon the
loom itself, where naught is now weaved.
With darkened skin they press upon the
grooves and think nothing of their own
fate as long as the impoverished perish
```

first. Allow me then, to linger on behind high walls and ramparts, lingering on the fruitless labours of the dead and spouting forth from the Tower of Babel curiosities and noise that does and shall come to naught. And such furious noise, such lamentable cries and deepest protestations in this dire tomb. For now, let it be said that the marks did not make themselves and the knives did not fashion their own designs."

- Earl Wathmere, BUS Radio

See what we mean? Someone fetch the straight-jacket!

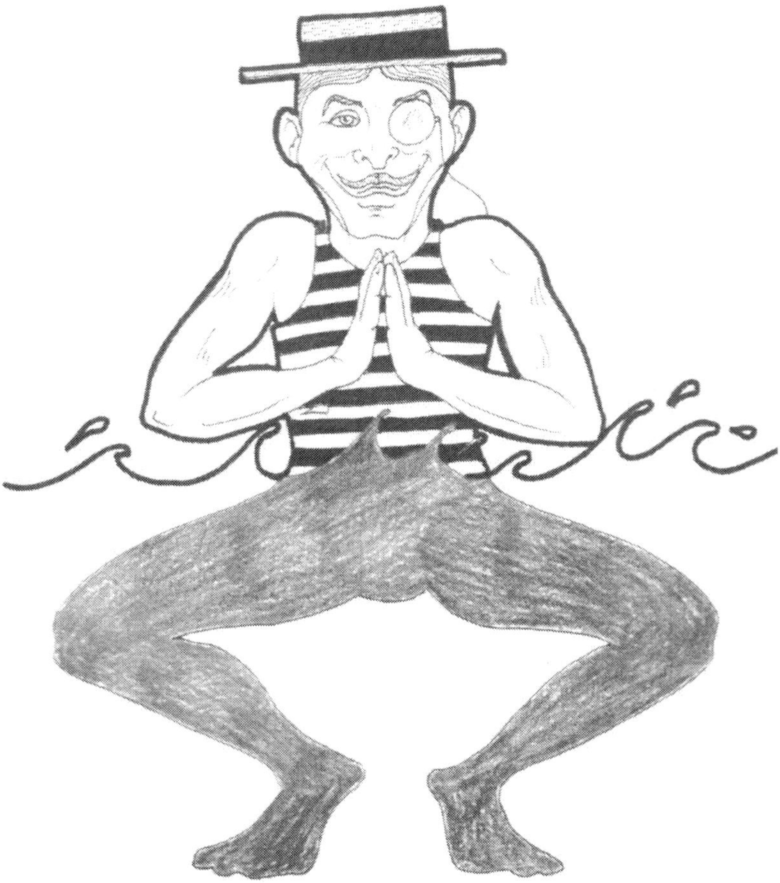

Excerpt from the MOS sponsored radio show 'The Adventures of Jack Jones'.

Narrator:
Ladies and gentleman, the adventures of Jack Jones (title music; audience applause). Jack is hiding in an abandoned house, on the run from three of your worst khaki-clad squaddies armed to the teeth with rifles and bayonets.

Soldier 1:
'Ere come on lads, he couldn't have got far, he's in here somewhere.

Soldier 2:
How dare he run from us? I'm going to run him through when I get hold of him.

Soldier 3:
Keep quiet you two, he could be armed.

(Tapping noise)

Soldier 1:
'Ere, did you hear that? It's coming

from the cellar.

Soldier 2:
Quick!

Narrator:
The three squaddies run down into the cellar to finish off our hero, but wait, lucky Jack is craftier than that! As the soldiers enter the stone cellar, Jack appears at the top of the stairs (audience applause).

Jack:
Whatcha' guv (audience laughter).

Soldier 1:
How the bloody hell did you do that, the sound came from down here!

Jack:
'Ere I'm Jack Jones, don't you know? I won't give away my secrets for forty shillings on the King's drum (audience laughter).

Soldier 2:
Quick, grab him.

Narrator:
Jack Jones is too smart for these brigands though, and quickly closes the metal door and locks it, trapping the three soldiers below in an empty, windowless, stone cellar (audience applause).

Jack:
Always have a backup plan. That's what you get for messing with 'Lucky Jack' lads.

Soldier 1:
That's it, we'll shoot our way out.

Jack:
Are you having a bubble bath? (Audience laughter) You've had no bullets in those guns for months.

Soldier 3:
There's no perishing way of getting out of this ruddy mess.

Jack:
You should have read this handy handbook (audience applause).

Soldier 1:
Looks like we're brown bread.

Jack:
If you were brown bread I'd butter you myself (audience laughter). I'll give you three days before you're goners, see you then!

Soldier 2:
Come back you rogue! Come back!

Jack:
Whatcha' (audience laughter).

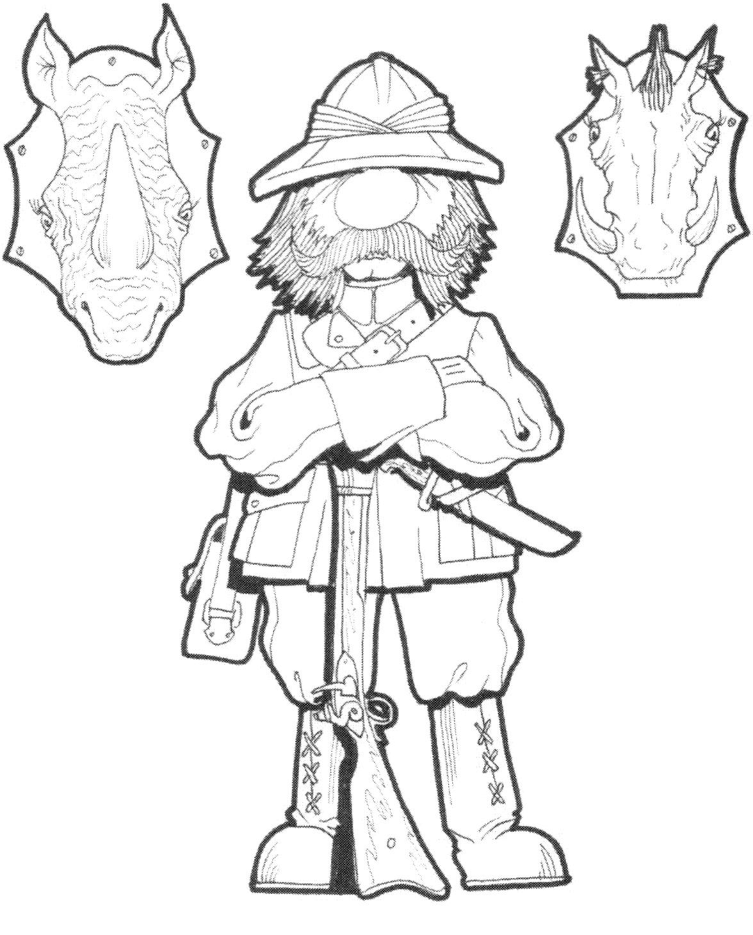

FOOD · IN SHANGRI-LA

"The sluggard does not plough after the autumn, so he begs during the harvest and has nothing."
– Proverbs 20:4; Church of the Remnant

Shangri-La

We've already touched on the concept of Shangri-La, and we won't bang on about it, as we don't want to give you false hope. However, we truly do hope that many of you Citizen Survivors do find your own Shangri-La. We can't say anymore on this, you'll know it when you find it. That precious corner of Blighty that can be your own, away from bully denizens, mad townies, the Church of the Remnant and squaddies and coppers. It's a long shot, improbable but not impossible! Man needs something to strive for.

Let us hold on to hope and assume you have or will soon find your Shangri-La. If you have, well, good for you! You've managed what most people have died trying for! It may not be forever, but it's for now, and that is good enough. Time to make a home.

All you have learnt so far will still be relevant, so it will never be a case of resting on your laurels, but at least you can give your feet a rest and thinking about settling down, and to do that you'll need to grow and preserve your own food.

Forager to farmer

Once you have survived hiking in your search for Shangri-La, the next natural progression is to start to consider a long term plan. The plan must take into account whether you will be remaining in your new home for a decent period of time, and by decent we mean a couple of years at least.

In just about any situation, it may be necessary to move about in order to avoid being compromised. If that's the case, then the long term growing of food has to be even more carefully considered. But it is more than possible to successfully grow your own food for survival with a long term plan.

If you intend to move about to avoid detection then it is still possible to start the beginnings of a food source with seeds that are both hardy and will reproduce naturally with the very minimum of human intervention and help. These 'crops' can be left to grow naturally and can even form part of a food cache that you can come back to – remember, vegetables and crops will find a way to grow naturally. So with the minimum amount of help from yourself they will do quite well anyway.

Basic farming and growing methods are an essential survival skill to learn – even the very basic methods will produce food that is more than acceptable to eat. As Citizen Survivors, long term food supplies are often overlooked, but it is actually a very essential part of your new life.

The good part is that we can prepare very easily – seeds are small, compact and lightweight, everything a Citizen Survivor wants. You can hold a vast supply of seeds that will produce food in abundance for you, year in, year out – you just have to be prepared with a stash. If not, why not try scrumping a garden store? We can't imagine many bully denizens heading that way!

Growing your own food
There are many reasons to grow your own food other than for pure survival and cutting down on hunting and scrumping time. Longevity is the main reason Citizen Survivors should farm their gardens to produce fresh fruit and vegetable for years to come. Just about anyone can have a crop of vegetables regardless – you can grow something. It's all possible and will add a bit of variety to your supper. Don't misinterpret this to mean we condone staying put with the townies though!

Whether it's growing tomatoes out on the porch or cucumbers on the windowsill, potatoes at the end of the balcony or some runner beans climbing up the south wall, producing your own food is the key to staying alive. Growing your own food is beneficial to you and your family, and will help you survive the situation we are all in.

In some countries there is only a short growing season, typically Northern Europe and Africa. This means adapting to your environment and growing the quicker producing vegetable varieties, ones that can be easily harvested and then stored for the winter. In many other areas there are true growing seasons allowing plenty of time for planting and harvesting

You may not be blessed with good, nutrient-rich soil – the type that will give you excellent yields of crops – so, depending on your particular soil, it may be necessary to just plant essential crops and do without the more luxurious foods until you have fertilised and worked the areas. Plants will simply not grow and thrive with low levels of rainfall – most food crops will need substantial amounts of water. You must certainly consider the amounts of normal rainfall in your area. From there you can decide if you will be needing added irrigation from your stored water.

The amount of crops you can grow in your home or garden will always be limited to the planting area available to you. In your situation you may well have a lot more room for your crops.

Food types
Are we boring you with all this talk of gardening and farming? Not very Jack Jones, is it? But you're a Citizen Survivor, about to dig for victory and reap your rewards. Let's think vegetables then.

Vegetables: This includes leafy vegetables, root vegetables, legumes, corn and vining vegetables like cucumbers, melons, squash, and pumpkins. These vegetables will give you many of the essential nutrients and vitamins you need to survive, and include:

- Proteins. Legumes are an extremely good and a high source of your protein.
- Carbohydrates. Potatoes and beets contain complex carbohydrates, a good source of energy as well as minerals.
- Vitamins and minerals. Most of the leafy vegetables, like lettuce or cabbage, as well as the vining vegetables like cucumbers and squash, provide an excellent means of obtaining the essential vitamins and minerals your body will require for added assimilation of the proteins, plus general good health

Fruits: Easily eaten and requiring little preparation or cooking, fruit is an excellent source of vitamin C. It is also a great food as it can (in theory) be canned or dehydrated for future use.

Grains: Of all the foods you can grow yourself, grains are probably the most important – grains were the staple food of most of the world's diet. Very rich in energy giving carbohydrates and fibre, they can be mixed with most other foods to give a substantial meal. Grains have the added advantage of the fact that they can be easily stored for long amounts of time, making them an ideal Citizen Survivor food. There is a great difference in growing seasons with grains, as well as summer and winter varieties of many of these. Generally speaking, summer grains, such as corn and summer wheat, are planted near the end of winter when freezing temperatures are not expected to continue for more than a few weeks, and they take about 110 days to mature, then another 30-60 days to dry sufficiently to harvest for storing as seed.

Corn: Often eaten as a vegetable with meals, corn is also a versatile grain that can be stored whole, unshucked, shelled (removed from the cob, with whole kernels), or ground into meal for use in making breads or mush dishes like grits. Corn is probably the easiest grain to grow for the novice farmer.

Wheat: Most people are familiar with wheat, from which we used to get most of our flour for baking everything from breads to cakes and pastries. Wheat stores well after harvest, but harvesting itself is more laborious than it is for corn, since the whole plant is usually cut down, sheaved (placed in piles), gathered and threshed (beaten to free the seeds), and ground into flour.

Oats: Another grain, oats for human consumption are processed more than wheat or corn, and the labour involved in harvest is equal to wheat. Still, it may be considered an option in some areas where it is easily grown.

Beans, peas, and other legumes: These are planted after the threat of frost, and require 75 to 90 days to produce fruit, which can continue producing as long as the plants are cared for until autumn frost.

Gourds: This group of plants includes squash, melons, and pumpkins, and is planted after the last expected frost, and takes between 45 days (cucumbers) to 130 days for pumpkins, to produce harvestable fruit.

Tomatoes: This fruit can be planted in many ways, from straight in the soil to hanging baskets and various containers. If kept warm, and transplanted into soil after the threat of frost, they will also produce season-long as well. Tomatoes, of course, are highly nutritious and can also be preserved.

Orchard fruits: Apples, pears, plums, and peaches are regarded as orchard fruits in most places, and do not require annual planting. The trees that bear these fruits require pruning and maintenance and usually take 2-3 years before producing their first, modest crop. When the trees begin producing fruit, the yield should increase yearly, and after they become mature and established, a single tree can produce bushels of fruit each year.

Planning your farm
Develop a farm plan on the land you intend to use for your food production. List all of the possible crops you will attempt to cultivate on your land. You should try to have as diverse a selection of vegetable growing plants as possible to meet nutrition requirements. If you have lots of room, plant an excess to allow for poor performance until you have a firm grasp of what you are doing.

Plan to use your land as effectively as possible if you are limited in space. Except in very cold regions, you may expect to be able to grow and harvest summer, autumn, winter, and spring crops. This will allow you to enjoy some fresh produce year around. Beets, carrots, cauliflower, snow peas, cabbage, onions, turnips, collards, mustard greens, and many other vegetables actually prefer growing in cold weather if the ground does not freeze. Winter crops are also much less subject to insect problems. If you are very tight on space, consider your alternatives

Breaking the ground
Breaking the ground, this is simply the process of loosening the soil, and "turning under", or covering, the plants or plant residue from a previous crop. It may also be referred to as "tilling", and is done with a plough.

On a small plot of land or if you can't scrump what you need, you may have to revert to the use of pick, shovel and hoe. This can be accomplished collectively. You should clear away any large stones, roots and limbs, heavy accumulation of vegetation, and other debris before tilling.

Maintaining your farm
Mark out the area you intend to plant, and with a hoe or plough, create a slightly raised bed in the loose soil in a line across the length of the plot. Next, make your furrow (a shallow groove cut in the soil) with your chosen implement.

Place your seeds in the furrow at the depth required for the particular crop you are planting. This may vary according to your choice of plants. As a rule, succulent plants like legumes (beans and peas) and melons, squash, cucumbers are planted between ¾ and 1 inch

(2 – 2.5 cm) deep, where corn and potatoes may be planted 2½ to 3½ inches (6.3 – 9 cm) deep. After placing the seed in the furrow, cover them and tamp (gently pack down) the soil lightly so the seed bed (the covered furrow) does not dry out as quickly. Continue this process until you have the number of rows you planned on planting.

Because you are planting this crop in rows, you will be able to walk the centre area between rows (the middles) to accomplish this, if you are doing this by hand. You will want to keep the soil around the roots loosened without damaging the roots themselves. You may apply mulch to reduce, if not eliminate weeds or unwanted growth from undesirable plants.

Watch for insects and animals which may damage your plants. If you see leaves which have been eaten, you will have to determine what is causing the damage. Many animals find tender young plants in a garden more appetizing than native growth, so you will have to protect the plants from these, but insects are a much more prevalent problem with growing food. You may find you are able to keep insect damage to a minimum by simply removing and killing them as you find them.

Dig for victory!

You will have to educate yourself to some degree on when to harvest your crop. Many common garden vegetables are harvested as they become ripe, and continue to produce throughout the growing season with proper care. Grains, on the other hand, are most often harvested when they are fully ripened and dry on the plant. Harvesting is a labour intensive operation, and as you become experienced in growing, you will find that you need to reduce the production of some plants so that harvesting can be managed.

Surviving the winter

As you settle into your new life in Shangri-La, you will find your chores will be, quite simply, to survive and feed yourself and your family. Not bored are you? Not missing your adventures on the road? Remember why you were on the road in the first place, this is as good as it gets! The longer you become accustomed to surviving the easier life will become.

As your journey as a Citizen Survivor continues, you will become far more skilled at hunting and trapping for food, at catching and skinning and cooking fish and animals. You will begin small farming plots and grow your own vegetables and crops – all skills that you should know and can improve on. But there are times during the year when there is an abundance of foods and other times when the land is bare and food is far harder to come across. It therefore makes sense to try and preserve as much of that food as you can when it's in abundance. You must prepare for the lean times.

Sometimes it may not be possible to even hunt for your food. When this happens you must have the skills to preserve and store the foods that you have caught in the good times of the year. Building up a supply of food for the 'bad' times of the year is essential for all Citizen Survivors. There are many ways to increase the life of your food and make your food safe as well.

Learning how to naturally preserve your food will help you for ever.

Of course, as a Citizen Survivor, it is important to already be preserving your own foods in the home – you can make very effective food stores that have a good shelf life in your own kitchen right now – and you should prioritise doing this to help build up your food supplies.

Preserving food
It's all very well pottering in the garden when it's a warm sunny day; just look at you lazing about! Don't get complacent and forget the horrors that are still out there though! Are you ready for winter? What are you going to eat then? For common vegetables, you have several choices for storing them through the non-growing season. Carrots, turnips and other root vegetables can be stored well into the winter months by being clamped up. Drying produce is one option for long term preservation of meats, fruits, and vegetables, and for seed type crops like legumes, this will give excellent results.

Drying (or dehydration): This is a useful method for storing fruits and some vegetables. It can be done in most fairly dry, warm climates.

Canning: This requires containers (which are reusable with the exception of lids, which may deteriorate over time) but does require proper preparation, cooking equipment and skill.

Bedding. This is a method for storing root crops such as potatoes, rutabagas, beets, and other root crops. It is accomplished by layering the product in a dry, cool, location in a straw bed.

In Ground Storage: Many root crops and cole crops can be overwintered in the garden. In most cases it is important to prevent the ground from freezing. Milder winter climates may only need a frost blanket. But colder climates may need mulch of up to a foot and a plastic covering. This type of storage is an effective way to save space and keep your produce fresh.

Excerpt from the MOS sponsored radio show 'The Adventures of Jack Jones'.

Narrator:
Unfortunately, ladies and gentleman, due to unforeseen and extremely tragic circumstances, 'The Adventures of Jack Jones' has been cancelled indefinitely with immediate effect. Please leave the auditorium in a calm and orderly fashion. So long, cheerio and farewell to one and all.

('Who's gonna take you home tonight' by Jack Payne plays)

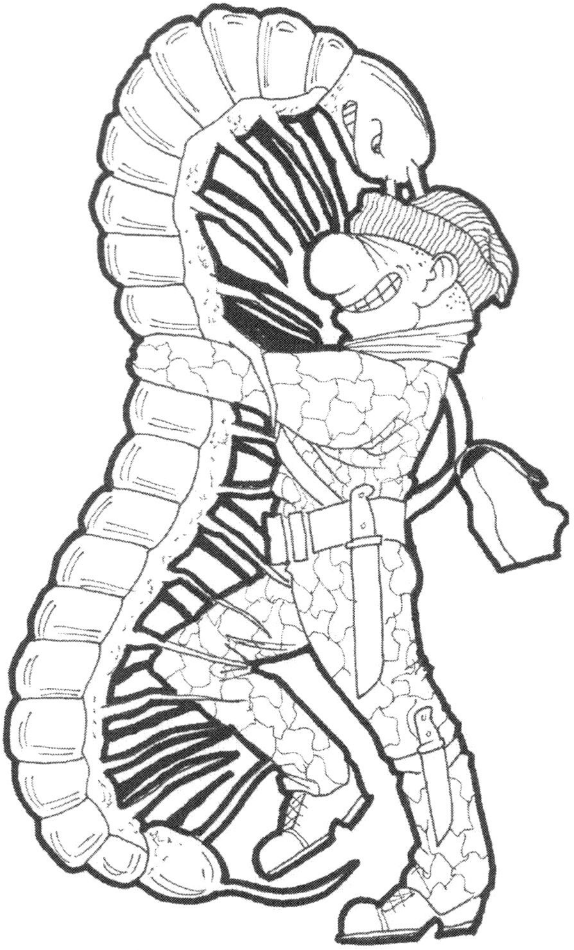

JOURNEY'S END

"He will wipe away every tear from their eyes, and death shall be no more, neither shall there be mourning, nor crying, nor pain anymore, for the former things have passed away."
– Revelation 21:4; Church of the Remnant

Some sunny day
Well Citizen Survivor, you've done it, you've survived. You truly have beaten the odds, with a good old bit of stiff upper lip and can-do spirit, you've rolled your sleeves up and carved out a little corner of Blighty for yourself. Take a moment to take it all in, you may even find a snifter of whiskey lying about, we'll look the other way - you've earnt it!

You've probably still got hundreds of questions. How to interact with other Citizen Survivors, territorial disputes, home security (particularly if you've got no bleedin' lock on the front door of your new home), black-out blinds, boarding up windows and countless others. Look, we've got you to Shangri-La, what do you want us to do? Should we pop round for a cuppa to come and visit your home ourselves? We've got you here, be grateful for once in your life.

What happens next is your choice. We've got you to

Shangri-La, and that was our intention, we're happy with that at least. Quiet isn't it? Birds singing, wind rustling through the trees. It's an awfully silent world without all that human noise.

What are you going to do now? Do you want to form a pack (join up with other people), do you feel you have met like-minded people you can commune and trade with? Do you want to risk starting a family or do you fancy yourself King of Port Isaac? Whatever you do next, the future is in your hands, with your new found Citizen Survivors you will now walk a path untrodden.

Finally, dear reader, let us dare to hope that Blighty can endure. This will be no mean feat and will require your constant vigilance, alertness and self-confidence. Carry it through, Citizen Survivor, however irksome it appears, with courage and determination. The more thorough we are now, the less likely are we to have trouble in the future.

Although now, at the close of this book, we feel it politic to confess one thing, to unburden our hearts of one dark and terrible secret, and that is [Omitted by order of the MOS].

Just remember – stay away from London!

Chin up, cheerio and carry on!

Thank you, good bye and good luck!

Witford Radio – 1570kHz MW
Putting the spunk back in Blighty

John McCormack – Keep the Home Fires Burning

George Formby – When I'm Cleaning Windows

Stanley Lupino and Elsie Carlisle - I Don't Want to Go to Bed

Jack Buchanan - Everything Stops for Tea

Flannagen and Allen – Umbrella Man

Henry Hall - The Sun Has Got His Hat on

Elsie Carlisle – Alone and Afraid

Bill Murray - I Wonder Who's Kissing Her Now

Binnie Hale - A Nice Cup of Tea

Jack Hylton - When You're Smiling

Gerald Adams – After the Ball

Harry Champion - I'm Henery the Eighth, I Am

Elsie & Doris Waters – Knees Up Mother Brown

Charles Coborn – Two Lovely Black Eyes

Bert Ambrose – One Hour with You

Jack Hylton – Button up Your Overcoat

Ronald Frankau – Fanny Is Evacuated Now

Courtland and Jeffries - Oh It's a Lovely War

Leslie Sarony – Why Build a Wall Round a Graveyard

Al Bowlly – Guilty

Flanagan and Allen – Hometown

Sam Browne – The King Is Still in London

Al Bowlly – Goodnight Sweetheart

Gracie Fields – Wish Me Luck as You Wave Me Goodbye

Henry Hall – Who's Afraid of the Big, Bad Wolf

Printed in Great
Britain
by Amazon